Study Guide to accompany Purtill's LOGIC

Study Guide to accompany Purtill's LOGIC: Argument, Refutation, and Proof
by Thomas J. McKay
Syracuse University

Harper & Row, Publishers
New York Hagerstown Philadelphia San Francisco London

Study Guide to accompany Purtill's LOGIC: Argument, Refutation, and Proof
Copyright ⓒ 1979 by Thomas J. McKay

ISBN 0-06-385439-2

CONTENTS

PREFACE

This study guide consists of section by section summaries of the material on deductive logic in Richard Purtill's Argument, Refutation and Proof, together with many examples that will provide important additional opportunities to apply the concepts introduced in that text.

By following the instructions that appear (in reduced type) in the study guide (as on the bottom of this page), you can use this as a guide to the main text. Alternatively, an instructor may wish to make specific assignments based upon the examples in the study guide, and the summaries can be used for review prior to exams.

At the end of each chapter of the study guide, answers are given for many (sometimes all) of the examples. In studying logic it is extremely important to write the answers for each set of examples before checking at the end of the chapter. Successful study requires that you work out each example yourself. Checking the answers and then figuring out how they were produced is no substitute for trying to apply the principles to arrive at the answer yourself.

In the early chapters (Chapters One and Three), where it is especially valuable to see a variety of examples completely worket out, the solutions for almost every problem in the chapter are included. Later there are generally answers for the odd-numbered examples alone.

Most of the examples in this study guide are somewhat simpler than those in the text, and they will provide an opportunity to check for mastery of the concepts before moving on to more difficult applications. A few are more difficult, and their mastery is not required for a basic understanding of the material in the text. They are marked by an asterisk (*).

> You should now begin by reading the opening paragraphs
> of Chapter One of the main text and the section entitled
> "Proofs and Refutations." When you have completed this
> reading, begin Chapter One of this study guide.

CHAPTER ONE

ARGUMENTS: PROOFS AND REFUTATIONS

      In giving an argument, one intends to support some conclusion or to refute
some claim.

      When an argument supports its conclusion, we call the argument a "proof."
For example,

            The Republicans will make significant gains in
            the upcoming elections, because almost every-
            one is disappointed with the Democratic policies.

The premise that almost everyone is disappointed with Democratic policise is given
as a reason to believe that the conclusion (that the Republicans will make significant gains) is true. If the premise were true, that would be good grounds for
accepting the conclusion.

      Sometimes an argument is intended to refute some claim that has been made.

            You are wrong to think that the Republicans
            will make significant gains. Scarcely any-
            one believes that they have adequate solutions
            for our present difficulties.

Here the premise (that scarcely anyone believes that they have adequate solutions
for our present difficulties) is put forward as a reason to disbelieve the claim
that the Republicans will make significant gains. Such an argument is called a
"refutation." In a refutation the premises support the negation of the refuted
statement.

      We must now develop the ability to tell when we have an argument, and to
determine what statement its premises are intended to support.

                              Exercise 1a

      Which of the following contain arguments? For each argument indicate what
statement (or statements) its premises are intended to support.

                                    1

1. It must be that hyenas are canines, because all of the scavengers of Africa are birds, felines or canines, and hyenas certainly are not birds or felines.

2. After a long hot day in a land rover, the sight of a pride of lions on the open plain lifts your spirits high.

3. Either Bob will bring binoculars or else Frank will be very angry, because if Bob doesn't bring them, no one will. But Frank always gets very angry if no one brings binoculars.

4. Since last summer, when he took his safari vacation, he has been a changed man.

5. Since all birds have feathers and Kiwis are birds, Kiwis must have feathers.

6. Those who say that all men oppose the principle of equal rights for women ignore the facts. Many prominent male senators, by the bills they have introduced or supported, have established themselves as firm supporters of women's rights.

7. I refuse to discuss this any further. You have no respect for my opinions, and anyway I'm sure I'm right.

8. If the governor is personally opposed to abortion, he should veto the bill.

9. The governor is personally opposed to abortion, so he should veto the bill.

10. The women's movement is wrong to try to establish equality. One or the other sex must dominate, and it would be socially disruptive to try to switch the positions of men and women.

> Answers to exercises appear at the end of each chapter.
> After checking your answers to Exercise 1a, read the
> next four sections of Purtill's text: "Validity and
> Invalidity," "Real-life Arguments," "Sound Arguments,"
> and "Reconstructing Arguments." Then proceed to the
> next section of this study guide before trying Exer-
> cise 1A in the text.

VALIDITY, INVALIDITY AND SOUNDNESS

After reading the first five sections of the text, you should be able to think more clearly about what it is for an argument to establish its conclusion.

A proof is deductively valid if the premises conclusively support (imply) the conclusion. If a proof is valid, then if its premises were true, its conclusion would have to be true as well.

A refutation is valid if the premises conclusively support the denial of the statement refuted. If the premises of the refutation were true, then the refuted statement would have to be false.

Validity is essential to proofs and refutations, but not all valid arguments are good arguments. Consider

> All dogs moo, and anything that moos can
> fly. So all dogs can fly.

This is valid, but it is unconvincing because we know that its premises are not true. To guarantee the truth of its conclusion a proof must be valid and have true premises. Such a proof is called "sound" proof. Similarly, a sound refutation is a valid refutation with true premises.

Validity is the logician's concern, but soundness rarely is. To determine whether an argument is sound, one must know something about its subject matter, and logic is concerned with the principles of reasoning common to all subject matters. Thus the logician rarely considers questions of soundness.

Exercise 1b

For each statement, indicate whether it is true or false.

1. Every valid proof has true premises and a true conclusion.

2. All invalid arguments have false premises.

3. Each sound proof has a true conclusion.

4. Every invalid argument has a false conclusion.

5. If a proof is deductively valid, then it is not possible for its premises to be true and its conclusion false.

6. If an argument is valid proof of a statement, then it is a valid refutation of the negation of that statement.

Exercise 1c

Which of the following are arguments? What is the conclusion of each argument? Which arguments are valid? For each valid argument, determine whether or not it is sound or explain why you cannot determine this.

1. All whales are mammals, and all mammals have lungs. So all whales have lungs.

2. All whales are birds and all birds have feathers. Therefore all whales have feathers.

3. Since all whales are birds and all birds have lungs, all whales must have lungs.

4. All whales have lungs. All animals larger than elephants have lungs. So all whales are animals larger than elephants.

5. All whales have an internal temperature greater than 25°C. Any animal with an internal temperature greater than 25°C must eat a weekly amount of food equal to at least 15% of its body weight, or else it loses weight. So any whale must eat a weekly amount of food equal to at least 15% of its body weight, or else it loses weight.

6. Whales have lungs, sharks have gills, and they are quite different in other ways as well.

7. At least some whales have gills, so, since no mammals have gills, not all whales are mammals.

8. All whales have lungs, but some can stay under water for more than an hour. So at least some creatures with lungs can stay under water for more than an hour.

9. Since some senators are lawyers and some senators are Republicans, some Republican senators are lawyers.

10. Not all senators have been elected, and some senators have been in office for many years. It does not follow that there are senators who have not been elected who also have been in office for many years.

11. If the President vetoes the bill, then it will not become law unless the lobbyists press hard for it. But if the lobbyists press hard for it, that will turn many senators against it. If many senators are turned against it, it will not become law. So if the President vetoes the bill, it will not become law.

> Now do Exercise 1A in the text, then read the section
> entitled "Logic and Language." After reading that
> section, return to the study guide.

LOGIC AND LANGUAGE

A proof consists of a series of <u>statements</u>, <u>premises</u> in support of a <u>conclusion</u>. In giving an argument, one <u>states</u> (asserts) the premises and the conclusion, and usually words like "so", "therefore", "hence", etc. indicate the conclusion or words like "since" and "because" indicate the premises.

The <u>indicative</u> sentence is the usual vehicle for making statements, and so most arguments consist primarily of indicatives. However, interrogatives, exclamations and imperatives can also be used to make statements (in a somewhat less direct way) and an argument can be given with these other forms of sentence.

Exercise 1d

In each case, indicate whether there is an argument. If there is, rewrite it using indicatives and clearly indicate the conclusion.

1. Must we decide whether it was stupidity or deliberate dishonesty that generated the administration's disastrous foreign policy? Shouldn't we turn them out of office in either case?

2. The demonstrators, who did not have a permit, were arrested. Can there be any question about the propriety of such arrests?

3. I believe that all people should have equal rights, yet I know that not all are treated in the same way by our laws and institutions. We must do something to correct this!

4. Benjamin Franklin was right: "A penny saved is a penny earned." Governmental efficiency is the key to what we all desire - lower taxes.

5. No taxation with representation!

4

Now do Exercise 1B in the text and then read the
section "Deduction and Induction." Before doing
Exercise 1C in the text, read the next section of
the study guide.

DEDUCTION AND INDUCTION

Many arguments that are not deductively valid provide strong but not absolutely
conclusive support for their conclusions. These are <u>inductive</u> arguments. If I
argue as follows,

> Since a certain style of art existed in ice
> age Europe and ice age Asia, there must have
> been some contact between the people of these
> areas.

then I am arguing inductively, since it is at least <u>possible</u> that these styles
developed independently, without such contacts. An argument intended to give
strong but not conclusive support to its conclusion is <u>inductive</u>.

In Chapters Eight and Nine probability theory is used to develop a rigorous
account of inductive argument. For now, keep in mind that in a <u>deductively</u> valid
argument, it is <u>absolutely impossible</u> for the premises to be true and the conclusion
false. Any degree of support less than that is not deductive.

Exercise 1e

For each of the following, indicate whether there is an argument, what the
conclusion is if there is one, and whether the premises are intended to support the
conclusion inductively or deductively.

1. All horses are mammals, so every horse's head is the head of some mammal.

2. His fingerprints are the only ones on the murder weapon. He must have
    committed the crime.

3. Everyone received a 5% raise, and last year Jones was making $20,000.
    So next year he will make $21,000.

4. Frank will study only if Bill helps him. But if he doesn't study, he
    won't pass. So Frank won't pass without Bill's help.

5. The row of apple trees and the overgrown lilac bush indicate that this
    plot of land was once inhabited.

6. The weatherman said that a low pressure system is moving in, and that it
    will soon rain. Since the sky is becoming very overcast, we can be sure
    that it will soon rain.

7. The President will sign the bill only if he is sure it will not be strictly
    enforced. He will be sure of that only if he appoints his own man to head
    the agency. So if the President signs the bill, he will appoint his own
    man to head the agency.

8. Dr. Smith believes that a tendency toward alcoholism can be an inherited
    physiological trait. Almost all of his alcoholic patients have had blood
    relatives who were also alcoholics.

9. My car is running perfectly. I'll be able to drive it for at least another year.

10. Every crow I've ever seen has been black, so all crows must be black.

Go on to Exercise 1C in the text, then complete the reading of Chapter One. Supplementary material on puzzles and on logical truths follows in the study guide.

MORE PUZZLES

Exercise 1f*

1.* If our senses do not deceive us, scientific theory is true. If scientific theory is true, our senses deceive us. What can we conclude from this?

2.* Our explorer meets three natives and wonders which are Abs and which Bas. The three natives, Abba, Dabba and Doo, are happy to "give him some information".
     Abba: We're all Bas.
     Dabba: No we're not. Only two are Bas.
     Doo: Abba and Dabba are both wrong.
How many are Abs (truth-tellers) and how many are Bas (false-speakers)? Which is which?

3.** Our explorer has been invited to stay for dinner. He can avoid being the main course if he can determine, after just one question, which of the king's hands is holding the small but priceless tribal jewel. But he doesn't know whether he is visiting the Abs or the Bas! What question should he ask the king?

4.** The tribal religion relies upon a book of revelations. The priest says that the following has been revealed to him:
     (R) R is not a revealed truth.
Should the priest add it to the book of revelations?

5.** The tribal witch-doctor treats some of the people of the village. In fact, of those who live in the village, he treats all and only the people who do not treat themselves. Where does the witch-doctor live?

LOGICAL TRUTHS

Every dog is a dog.

Every dog that barks is a dog.

Every dog that barks barks.

If Al and Bob are both tall, then Al is tall.

If every horse is a mammal, then everything eaten by a horse is eaten by some mammal.

If you love no one who loves himself, then you do not love yourself.

Those are logical truths. There is an easy way to list more. For example:

Every chair is a chair.

Every chair that is brown is a chair.

Every chair that is brown is brown.

If Charlie and Doug are both blonds, then Charlie is a blond.

If every shark is a fish, then everything chewed by a shark is chewed by some fish.

If you hit no one who hits himself, then you do not hit yourself.

Exercise 1h*

1. Make a list of six other logical truths, the easy way. (Use the patterns employed above.)

2. Now make a list of six logical truths that have a different pattern from those already listed.

7

1a 1. Conclusion: <u>Hyenas are canines</u>.
    2. No argument.
    3. Conclusion: <u>Bob will bring binoculars or Frank will be very angry</u>.
    4. No argument. 'Since' is used to indicate time or causation, not as an indicator of a premise.
    5. Conclusion: <u>Kiwis have feathers</u>.
    6. Supported: <u>Not all men oppose the principle of equal rights for women</u>.
        Refuted: <u>All men oppose the princple of equal rights for women</u>.
    7. No argument (in the logicians'sense of 'argument').
    8. No argument.
    9. Conclusion: <u>The governor should veto the bill</u>. In 8, there is a conditional statement made up of two other statements connected by 'if_____, then...'. But neither of the constituents is asserted. In 9, each is asserted and one is given as a reason for the other.
    10. Conclusion: <u>The women's movement is wrong to try to establish equality</u>. There is also a sub-argument with the conclusion: <u>Equality would not serve the interests of justice</u>. That conclusion serves as a premise to support the main conclusion.

1b 1. F. 'All whales are fish, and all fish have gills. Therefore, all whales have gills.' Valid, false conclusion.
    2. F. 'All whales are mammals, and some mammals climb trees. Therefore, all whales climb trees.' Invalid, true premises.
    3. T.
    4. F. 'All whales are mammals, and some mammals swim. So all whales swim.' Invalid, true conclusion.
    5. T.
    6. T.

1c 1. Conclusion: <u>All whales have lungs</u>. Valid, sound.
    2. Conclusion: <u>All whales have feathers</u>. Valid, not sound.
    3. Conclusion: <u>All whales have lungs</u>. Valid, not sound.
    4. Conclusion: <u>All whales are larger than elephants</u>. Invalid.
    5. Conclusion: <u>Any whale must eat a weekly amount of food equal to at least 15% of its body weight, or it loses weight</u>. Valid. How do you find out if it is sound? Ask a biologist.
    6. No argument.
    7. Conclusion: <u>Not all whales are mammals</u>. Valid not sound. (Note that if this were sound it would <u>refute</u> the claim that all whales are mammals.)
    8. Conclusion: <u>At least some creatures with lungs can stay under water for more than an hour</u>. Valid. Sound? Ask a whale expert.
    9. Conclusion: <u>Some Republican Senators are lawyers</u>. Invalid.
    10. No argument. This is a statement that a certain argument is not valid. It is not an argument itself.
    11. Conclusion: <u>If the President vetoes the bill, it will not become law</u>. Valid. To know if it is sound you need to know what bill (and what president, etc.) is being discussed, and a lot about senators and lobbyists.

1d There can be some significant variation in the versions of these arguments. These are offered as samples.

    1. The administration's foreign policy is disastrous. It was generated by dishonesty or stupidity. In either case, we should turn them out. Therefore, we should turn them out.
    2. These demonstrators did not have a permit. Arrests of demonstrators who do not have a permit are legal arrests. Therefore, the arrests were legal.

3. All people should have equal rights. Not all have equal rights. Therefore the situation is not correct. Let us correct it! (The last is a
   call to action based upon the recognition of the incorrect situation.)
4. If the government were more efficient, it would save money. If it saved
   money, it would not need to earn so much through tax revenue. Therefore,
   if the government were more efficient, we could have lower taxes.
5. We are not represented. Those who are not represented should not be
   taxed. So we should not be taxed.

1e. 1. Conclusion: Every horse's head is the head of some mammal. Deductive.
        (Valid.)

    2. Conclusion: He committed the murder. Deductive.

    3. Conclusion: Next year he will make $21,000. Deductive. (Valid.)

    4. Conclusion: Frank won't pass without Bill's help. Deductive. (Valid.)

    5. Conclusion: This plot of land was once inhabited. Inductive.

    6. Conclusion: It will soon rain. Inductive.

    7. Conclusion: If the president signs the bill, he will appoint his own man
        to head the agency. Deductive. Valid.

    8. Argument reported here. Conclusion: A tendency toward alcoholism can be
        an inherited, physiological trait. Inductive.

    9. Conclusion: I'll be able to drive my car for at least another year.
        Inductive.

   10. Conclusion: All crows are black. Inductive.

1f. 1. Our senses deceive us.

    2. Dabba is an Ab. Abba and Doo are Bas. (They can't all be wrong, so
        Abba is wrong. If Abba is wrong, Dabba is right, so Doo is wrong.)

    3. "If I asked you if the jewel was in the right hand, would you answer 'yes'?
        What should he do if they answer "Yes"? What if they answer "No"? Why
        does this work even if he doesn't know which tribe it is? "

    4. If he adds it, he will be adding something that is not a revealed truth.
        If R is true it is not a revealed truth, and if R is not true it is not
        a revealed truth.

    5. Outside the village. For suppose he lives inside the village. Then if
        he treats himself he doesn't treat himself. But if he doesn't treat
        himself, then he treats himself. Each case is contradictory if he lives
        in the village.

CHAPTER TWO

In the text read the first portion of Chapter
Two (on fallacies), up to Exercise 2A.

FALLACIES

An argument is legitimately persuasive for a person if it has premises the
person has good reason to accept, if those premises support the conclusion, and
if the conclusion is not already accepted. A <u>fallacious</u> argument has questionable
premises or premises that fail to support the conclusion. In addition, an argument
will fail to be persuasive if the conclusion is already believed just as strongly
as the premises (or to put this the other way around, it will fail to be persuasive
if the premises are just as questionable as the conclusion).

Not the Point

In <u>Not the Point</u> fallacies the premises do not support the conclusion and,
in fact, have only a vague connection with it. Perhaps the most striking thing
about such arguments is the fact that attitudes and opinions are sometimes changed
by them.

The traditional fallacy of <u>ad hominem</u> argument, for example, consists in
missing the point by attacking an individual who holds an opinion (or gives an
argument). The opinion (or argument) is never directly considered.

> We don't need to pay any attention to what
> Representative Major says about fiscal policy
> any longer. He was caught out on the town
> with that stripper Froo-froo Labanza.

As political advice this may be practical. But if it is an argument that Represen-
tative Major's views on fiscal policy have no merit, it is not to the point.

Many arguments that commit Not the Point fallacies can be identified by their
use of devices to change our attitude towards something without giving us any
relevant information. Advertisements that promote a car on the basis of its being
"precision-sized", for example, tell us absolutely nothing about the car. (What
could "precision-sized"mean?) They try to promote a favorable association without
giving us any information that would be relevant to our decision about what to purchas

Beside the Point

In <u>Beside the Point</u> fallacies, the premises do not support the conclusion though they do support something at least vaguely similar. Suppose the prosecuting attorney at a criminal trial says:

> If no one is punished for this horrible crime, we
> will not be able to rest in our beds.

He may be pointing out something true that could serve as a basis for concluding that vigorous police work is in order until the matter is settled. This is not, however, relevant to establishing that the defendant at the trial is guilty of committing the crime in question.

Beyond the Point

In <u>Beyond the Point</u> fallacies there is usually an unacceptable premise (sometimes an implicit premise) that is needed to make the set of premises adequate to support the conclusion. Sometimes a Beyond the Point fallacy occurs because the conclusion is already as acceptable as (or even the same as) one or more premises.

Few people would find an argument of the following sort to be persuasive.

> Since a fetus cannot have legal rights, we cannot
> prohibit abortion.

Anyone who is wondering about the truth of the conclusion will probably find the premise just as unacceptable. Such an argument will be rhetorically ineffective because it assumes as much as it establishes.

> Do Exercise 2A and 2B, then read the rest of
> Chapter Two (concerning weak arguments). Be-
> fore doing Exercise 2C, read the rest of
> Chapter Two of this study guide.

WEAK ARGUMENTS

Some arguments give us a good reason to accept a conclusion without giving us an absolute guarantee that the conclusion is true. However, the degree to which such arguments support their conclusion varies, and we must be careful not to accept them if the degree of support is not sufficiently high.

Argument from Authority

To accept the testimony of relevant authorities that there are particles smaller than atoms or that smoking is often injurious to health is very reasonable. Recognized authorities are in general agreement about these issues.

My cousin claims that my taking aspirin daily would prevent colds. A physics professor at my university says that more than eighty basic types of sub-atomic particle will be discovered. Power company spokesman assure us of the safety of nuclear plants. Accepting these claims without further question would be much less reasonable. My cousin is no expert and has little evidence. The physics professor is an authority, but here he is giving his view on a matter concerning which there is considerable disagreement among authorities; his opinion does not represent the only reasonable conclusion from the evidence. The power company spokesman has good reason to present a conclusion that is at odds with some of the evidence; he is a biased participant.

When relying on authorities we must be prepared to examine their credentials, to consider the extent to which the experts agree, and to take their biases into account. This still gives us no guarantee of a correct conclusion, but it at least safeguards us from being misled in cases in which the person who offers us his opinion might not be presenting the best conclusion to be drawn from the relevant evidence. When we are relying on others to draw conclusions for us, we must examine their credentials with care.

Hypothesis

In accounting for facts we attempt to devise hypotheses (and, more generally, theories) that explain the facts in question. Many factors must be considered in weighing the degree of plausibility of these hypotheses, and we will have a very weak argument (at best) if we hypothesize too rashly.

One way to guard against this problem is to devise as many hypotheses as possible and to create tests (experiments) that will help in deciding among them. (Much scientific training is aimed at developing these skills). A general account of devising and justifying hypotheses and theories is required to give this more depth. This takes us into the domain of general epistemology and philosophy of science. (The material in Chapters 8 and 9 of Purtill's text is relevant in developing general guidelines for this.)

Now do the remaining exercises in the
following order: 2a, 2C, 2D, 2E, 2F.

Exercise 2a

For each of the following short arguments

   A)   Identify the conclusion

   B)   Indicate whether the premises support the conclusion. (That is, if
        I believed the premises, would I have good reason to accept the
        conclusion?)

   C)   In those cases involving fallacies or weak arguments, explain what
        the difficulty is.

1. Don't pay any attention to Smith's arguments against the national health plan.
   His wife is a doctor, so naturally he is opposed to anything that might put
   some controls on doctors' fees.

2. Most men who have never been married are obsessed with sex. This is to be
   expected, because that's how bachelors are.

3. The President will not be re-elected unless he is able to control the economy.
   But no matter what he does to control the economy he will lose the support of
   either business or labor, and if he loses the support of business or labor,
   he will not be re-elected. So the President will not be re-elected.

4. Philosophers of science are the ones to ask about the right way to interpret
   the equations of physics. Any philosopher will tell you that.

5. The President has assured us that our nation cannot survive without a strong
   military, and no one has demonstrated that he is wrong. So we must maintain
   our military strength.

12

6. Was it through stupidity or through deliberate dishonesty that the Administration botched its foreign policy? In either case, you should vote against the incumbents.

7. If you're not a reformed drunkard, then why don't you reform?!

8. Our organization is founded on two principles that are essential to the continued health of our society. First, that everyone must be required to work and contribute his share to the general welfare. Second, that the government should not force the people to do things, but should be their servant. The rest of our program is derived from these principles.

9. Murder is wrong, no matter who the victim is. We must stop the murder of unborn children.

10. Since the success of the women's movement is inimical to family cohesiveness, we must stop it now. Vote against the measures they support.

11. Question on government form sent to all universities: "What steps are you taking to eliminate past discrimination?"

12. Marijuana is often a healthful means to relaxation and pleasure. Since everyone has a right to relax, marijuana should be available to everyone.

13. The medical care bill must be a fraud because Senator Senior supports it and he's just a power-hungry politician.

14. Defense lawyer to jury: "This man was tormented by his wife for years. Shall we now add to that injury by convicting him of her murder?"

15. A senatorial speech: "I fail to see how anyone can oppose the national health care proposal. Are some senators opposed to good health? Have they polled their constituents and found a reservoir of sentiment in favor of illness? Let us return to our senses and vote in favor of national health care."

16. He has never been convicted of any crime, so I guess he has never committed one.

17. Senator Senior's record of attendance at roll-call votes is the best in the Senate. Since he works for you, won't you vote for him?

18. More people use Bleep! than any other brand.

19. Frank and Flo were just beginning their first meal on board the train. As the train entered a tunnel, Frank bit into his shrimp appetizer. He screamed to Flo, "Don't eat the food! It'll make you go blind!"

20. Everyone who takes Bleep! gets rid of his cold.

21. Most faculty members claim that without adequate salaries a high quality faculty cannot be maintained at this institution. But we have the example of several universities to show us that large increases in faculty salaries do not lead to a higher quality faculty.

22. The oil industry's argument against polution control should not be taken seriously, because they have a special interest in curbing such controls.

23. By bribing officials and by using subordinates to commit those crimes for which conviction would be likely, the major crime bosses in our country avoid being locked up. As long as we adhere to constitutional principles and standard practice concerning the admission of evidence in trials, we will never convict them. It is now imperative that we ignore those principles and practices in order to bring the menace of organized crime under control.

ANSWERS

2a. These should be viewed as starting points for discussion. Other answers may
     be plausible in some cases.

1.   Ad hominem. (Not the Point.)
3.   A valid argument.
5.   Appeal to authority where authorities do not agree. (Weak argument)
7.   Beyond the Point. (Assumes drunknenness.)
9.   Beyond the Point. (Assumes that abortion is murder, but this is the point
     at issue.)
11. Beyond the Point. (Assumes past discrimination.)
13. Ad hominem. (Not the Point.)
15. Beside the Point. (Should be arguing that this bill is the most appropriate
     way to promote health care goals.)
17. Beside the Point. (Attendance record is a poor indicator. At best, it
     is a necessary condition of good performance, not sufficient.)
19. Post hoc ergo propter hoc. Perhaps   ad hoc hypothesis.
21. Confuses enabling causes and effecting causes.
23. Beside the Point. The conclusion that we must ignore established principles
     in order to wipe out organized crime is not the same as the conclusion that
     we must ignore the established principles. Other factors are relevant.

CHAPTER THREE

In the text, begin Chapter Three and read through
the section "Disjunction and Cancellation." Then
return to the study guide.

STATEMENT LOGIC: THE SIMPLE SYSTEM

In Chapter Three we begin the study of the principles of deductive inference.
There are an infinite number of distinct deductive arguments, but there are a small
number of valid argument patterns which can be used, in a step by step manner, to
derive the conclusion of an argument whenever it validly follows from the premises
or to refute the conclusion whenever the argument is a valid refutation. By recognizing these and agreeing upon a deductive system based upon them, we can always
come to agreement about whether or not to accept a proposed derivation. We will
accept it if it is produced step by step in accord with the rules of our deductive
system.

Many arguments involve compound statements. These are statements that have
other statements as parts. For example,

The President will veto the bill or it will become law

consists of two statements.

The President will veto the bill

It (the bill) will become law

joined by the connective word "or".

In Chapters Three and Four we examine some of the ways in which compound
statements are constructed, and some of the inferences involving them.

One simple form of inference involving compound statements is known as
"simple cancellation" (or "disjunctive syllogism") . We are given, as premises,
that there are just two cases to consider and that one of those is ruled out. Thus
the other must obtain.

(I) The President will veto the bill or it will become law.
But the President will not veto it.
So the bill will become law.

15

Let's consider the components of arguments (I) . There are two simple statements in this argument.

> The President will veto the bill
> The bill will become law.

In the first premise, they are joined together by the word "or" to make a compound sentence. Compound statements consisting of statements joined by the word "or" (or equivalent connectives) we call "disjunctions".

Thus all of the following are disjunctions.

> I will take calculus or I will take physics.
> Al will do the job or he'll have someone do it for him.
> I will study on Saturday or I will go on a picnic on Saturday.

Many such sentences will be shortened in ordinary speech. For example

> I will take calculus or physics.
> On Saturday I will study or go on a picnic.

But these shorter sentences have the same meanings as the longer compound sentences given above, and they play the same role in inferences. (We will want to represent these in the same way as the more explicity compound statements.)

Notice that in the second premise of argument (I), we have the denial or negation of one of the constituents of the disjunction (of one of the disjuncts) .

> The President will not veto the bill

is the negation of

> The President will veto the bill.

Thus one alternative is ruled out, yielding our conclusion.

By using symbols to represent disjunction and negation, we can get a clearer, more succinct presentation of the pattern that argument (I) has in common with many others. We use capital letters to stand in place of statements and " v " to represent disjunction ("or"), and we abbreviate the first premise

> A v B   .

The second premise is the negation of the sentence standing on the left in the disjunction. To represent this we use "~" in front of the appropriate capital letter, thus

> ~A.

So the inference pattern employed here is

> A v B
> ~A
> ―――――
>   B   .

This is one form of simple cancellation.

There are an infinite number of valid arguments that have the pattern just exhibited.

> I will have to eat beef or chicken for dinner (A v B).
> But I won't eat beef (~A) , so I will have to eat chicken (B) .

It couldn't have been Peewee Reese who set the style for dixieland clarinet players (~A) . But it was either Peewee Reese or Peewee Russell (A v B) , so it must have been Peewee Russell (B) .

The rules must be changed or the champ will not fight (A v B) . Thus the champ will not fight (B) , because they won't change the rules (~A) .

(Construct a few examples yourself before continuing.)

In addition to the pattern given above, in which the left disjunct of one premise is negated in the other premise, the following will be regarded as versions of simple cancellation (SC) .

$$\frac{\begin{array}{l} A \ v \ B \\ \sim B \end{array}}{A} \qquad \frac{\begin{array}{l} \sim A \ v \ B \\ A \end{array}}{B} \qquad \frac{\begin{array}{l} A \ v \ \sim B \\ B \end{array}}{A}$$

(Notice how simple it is to present these in symbolic form.) In addition, this rule can be applied even with longer disjunctions. Thus

$$\frac{\begin{array}{l} A \ v \ B \ v \ C \\ \sim A \end{array}}{B \ v \ C}$$

is a legitimate version of SC, as is

$$\frac{\begin{array}{l} A \ v \ B \ v \ C \ v \ D \\ \sim D \end{array}}{A \ v \ B \ v \ C} \qquad .$$

DERIVATIONS

Even with just one rule we can begin to do derivations, in which we proceed step by step to <u>derive</u> the conclusion of an argument from its premises. Thus suppose that we have the argument

The Governor must win his court battles or he will be impeached. But either he won't win his court battles or else the court will be ignoring precedent. Since the court will not ignore precedent, he will be impeached.

We can symbolically represent that, using capital letters to represent the atomic sentences.

G# The Governor will win his court battles.
M# The Governor will be impeached.
C# The court will ignore precedent.

The argument then is

$$\frac{\begin{array}{l} G \ v \ M \\ \sim G \ v \ C \\ \sim C \end{array}}{M}$$

Even though this is not an instance of simple cancellation (SC) , we can employ that inference pattern to show that this is valid.

```
1.  G v M
2.  ~G v C
3.  ~C
4.  ~G        2,3 SC
5.  M         1,4 SC
```

We show first that if the premises are true, than "~G" must be true as well. Similarly, we show that if the premises and "~G" are true, "M" must be true. Thus we use SC in two separate steps to establish that if the premises are true than "M" must be true as well. This constitutes a derivation of the conclusion from the premises.

Exercise 3a

Determine which of these premises cancel out to the indicated conclusion, or to a refutation of the indicated statement. If they neither establish nor refute the indicated statement, write "NC".

```
1.  A v ~B            7.  A v B v C
    B       A?            ~A        B?

2.  ~A v C v D        8.  A
    A       C v D?        B         D?
                          ~B v C
                          ~A v ~C v D
3.  A v ~C
    C v ~D  D?       9.  ~B
    ~A                    B v ~A    D?
                          B v C
4.  ~A v B                A v ~C v D
    B       A?
                     10. A v ~B
5.  ~A v B v C            C v ~A    D?
    A       B?            ~D v ~A v ~C
    ~C                    B

6.  ~A v B
    ~B v C
    A v D   C?
    ~D
```

Now read the next three sections of the text, "Cancel and Collect," "Arguments with "if..., then...," and "Equivalence Rules." Then read the next section of the study guide.

ADDITIONAL RULES: CANCEL AND COLLECT

Before we can derive the conclusions of a much larger variety of arguments, we will need to agree upon additional simple inference patterns that we can use, like SC, as inference rules.

Consider the following argument.

I must flick the switch or else the alarm
will not sound. But I must move my arm, or
I won't flick the switch. So I must move
my arm or the alarm will not sound.

This is the pattern

$$F \lor \sim A$$
$$\underline{M \lor \sim F}$$
$$M \lor \sim A$$

which we will call "<u>cancel and collect</u>" (CC) . This too is a valid form of argument. A sentence and its negation "cancel each other out" and the remaining constituents are disjoined in a single sentence.

We can now do some more complex derivations. Consider this argument

> Bright-colored plumage in male birds aids
> in camouflage or helps in attracting predators away
> from the nest or else it is a result of sexual
> selection. It does not aid in camouflage. Female
> birds must be able to see color or else it is not
> a result of sexual selection. Thus either female
> birds can see color or else bright color in male
> birds helps in attracting predators away from the
> nest.

This would be represented

$$C \lor P \lor S$$
$$\sim C$$
$$\underline{F \lor \sim S}$$
$$F \lor P$$.

We can now derive the conclusion in steps

1.	C v P v S	
2.	~C	F v P?
3.	F v ~S	
4.	P v S	1,2 SC
5.	F v P	3,4 CC

using the two rules we have so far adopted for our system of deductive inference.

EQUIVALENCE RULES

    In addition to SC and CC it will be useful to have some <u>equivalence rules</u>
that allow the interchange of equivalent formulas. In the following simple argument

$$A \lor B \lor C$$
$$\underline{\sim A}$$
$$C \lor B$$

we have a conclusion that we could not derive using just SC (or CC) . Yet this
conclusion is clearly equivalent to "B v C", which is easily derived in a single
SC step from the premises. To allow the derivation of "C v B" we will introduce
an equivalence rule, commutation.

$$\underline{A \lor B}$$
$$B \lor A$$

Reversing the order of the disjuncts makes no difference in meaning. "A v B" and

19

"B v A" convey the same information and are entirely interchangeable in all arguments and within any sentence. We can now derive "C v B" in either of two ways

1.	A v B v C			1.	A v B v C		
2.	~A			2.	~A		
3.	B v C	1,2 SC		3.	A v C v B	1, Comm.	
4.	C v B	3, Comm.		4.	C v B	2,3 SC	

The second way employs the equivalence rule <u>within</u> a formula to derive a new formula. This is a perfectly legitimate use of equivalence rules. (There is no analogous legitimate use of inference rules like SC and CC which are not equivalence rules).

It will also be useful to have the equivalence rule "Double Negation" (DN) and the two equivalence rules "Repetition" (Rep).

$$\text{DN} \quad \frac{A}{\sim\sim A} \qquad\qquad \text{Rep} \quad \frac{A \lor A}{A} \qquad \frac{A}{\begin{array}{c}A\\A\end{array}}$$

DN allows the elimination (or introduction) of double negations, and Rep allows the elimination (or introduction) of redundant disjuncts in a formula or of redundant lines in a proof. Introduction of these rules will enable us to do a much larger variety of derivations.

Now do Exercise 3A in the text, then do exercise 3b
in this study guide.

Exercise 3b

Using the rules of SC, CC, Comm., DN and Rep., show that each of these is valid by deriving the conclusion from the premises.

1. A v B
    ~C v ~A
    ~E v C
    ‾‾‾‾‾‾‾
    ~E v B

2. A
    ~C v B
    ~A v C v D
    ‾‾‾‾‾‾‾‾‾
    B v D

3. ~A v B
    ~A v C
    ~E v ~C
    ‾‾‾‾‾‾‾
    ~A

4. ~A v C v D
    A
    ‾‾‾‾‾‾‾‾‾
    C v D

5. ~A v B v C
    ~B
    ‾‾‾‾‾‾‾‾‾
    ~A v C

6. A v B v C
    ~C
    ‾‾‾‾‾‾‾
    B v ~~A

7. ~A v B
    ~C v D
    A v C
    ‾‾‾‾‾
    B v D

8. ~A v F
    ~C v F
    A v C
    ‾‾‾‾‾
    F

9. ~A v B
    ~B v C
    ~B v D
    ‾‾‾‾‾‾‾‾
    ~A v C v D

10. A v B v C
    ~C v D
    ~B v D
    ‾‾‾‾‾
    A v D

Before doing 3B in the text, read the remainder of
Chapter 3 of the study guide.

REPRESENTING ENGLISH

English has many more types of statement compounds than just those constructed employing "or".

> If the President signs the bill, it will become law.
> The President is unhappy and the Secretary of State is furious.
> The President will not sign the bill, but it will become law anyway.
> The President will sign the bill only if he believes it is in the national interest.

Here the words "if", "and", "but", and "only if" are used (together with sentence negation) in the construction of compound statements from their atomic constituents. Using only the two symbols introduced so far, " v " and "~", we can represent the deductively relevant features of these compound statements. When we do so, we enable ourselves to evaluate arguments involving these statement compounds, and we need only the simple system for statement logic already developed.

"If"

Statements of the form "If A then B" are <u>conditional</u> statements. "A" is called the "<u>antecedent</u>" and B the "<u>consequent</u>" of the conditional. While such statements are usually used to indicate a connection, often a causal connection, between A and B, there is a more fundamental core that all conditionals share. If someone says "If A then B" he is at least committed to its <u>not</u> happening that A is true and B is false. In other words, either A is not true or B must be true. This is our basis for representing these statements.

> If A, then B

will be represented by

> ~A v B

A is not true or else B is true.

The following examples will indicate how this representation is done.

> If A̲l passes logic, he will be admitted to the advanced program in b̲iology.
>
> > ~A v B
>
> If Charlie does not go to the party, then Dave will not go either. (C# Charlie goes. D# Dave goes.)
>
> > ~~C v ~D
> >   or
> > C v ~D
>
> If Elmer eats that hamburger, then either Frank or George will have to have a hot dog. (E# Elmer eats. F# Frank has a hot dog. G# George has a hot dog)
>
> > ~E v F v G
>
> If the Senate passes the bill, then if the President signs it, it will become law. (S# Senate passes. P# President signs. L# It becomes law.)

21

~S v ~P v L

"And" and "But"

Compound statements of the form "A and B" are <u>conjunctions</u>. These statements are true precisely when each of the constituent statements "A" and "B" are true. In our simple system for statement logic, we will break up conjunctions and treat each of the constituents as a separate statement. A conjunction in the premises of an argument will be represented as two separate premises. A conjunction in the conclusion will be regarded as two separate conclusions each of which must be derived if validity is to be established.

> If <u>A</u>l passes, then if <u>B</u>ill passes too, then we can have quite a <u>p</u>arty in their honor. Al will pass if he <u>s</u>tudies, and Bill will pass if he <u>s</u>tudies, and both are studying, so I guess we'll have quite a party.

$$\begin{array}{ll} \sim A \text{ v} \sim B \text{ v} P & \\ \sim S \text{ v} A & P? \\ \sim T \text{ v} B & \\ \quad S & \\ \quad T & \end{array}$$

The word "but" is a sentence connective with the same deductive significance as "and". Any sentence compound "A but B" is true precisely when "A" and "B" are both true. Thus, as with "and", we will represent this by writing "A" and "B" as separate premises or separate conclusions. "Although", "despite the fact that" and many similar connectives also have the same deductive significance as "and".

> If the President <u>s</u>igns the bill it will become <u>l</u>aw, but if the pressure <u>g</u>roups go to work on the labor department it will not be strictly <u>e</u>nforced. The President will sign the bill, but the pressure groups will go to work on the labor department, so the bill will become law but it will not be enforced.

1.	~S v L	
2.	~G v ~E	L?
3.	S	~E?
4.	G	
5.	L	1,3 SC
6.	~E	2,4 SC

In this example we had two conclusions to establish. Similarly, if we wish to <u>refute a disjunction</u>, we must show that neither disjunct can be true. So here we will have to refute each disjunct.

> We won't have either the President or the opposition leader happy with this bill. This is because the President won't be happy with it if the lobbyists manage to get some <u>c</u>hanges made, and the opposition leader won't be happy with it if it is not significantly amended. But even though the lobbyists will manage to get some changes made, it will not be significantly amended.

1.	~C v P		4.	~S	
2.	~~S v ~O	P v O?	5.	~P	1,3 SC
3.	C		6.	~O	2,4 SC

22

Lines 5 and 6 are required to refute "P v O". We must rule out each case.

MORE ENGLISH CONNECTIVES

The English connective "<u>only if</u>" is sometimes troublesome. Consider

>   We will get to <u>M</u>ars only if we are technologically <u>p</u>roductive.

We will represent this by

>   ~M v P

or, equivalently

>   P v ~M.

This conveys the equivalent claim that

>   Either we will be productive or else we will not go to Mars.

Statements of the form "A if and only if B" make what we will regard as two separate claims, "A if B" and "A only if B". The first is represented

>   ~B v A

and the second

>   ~A v B   .

Thus the statement

>   The bill becomes <u>l</u>aw if and only if
>   the <u>P</u>resident signs it.

will be represented by the two statements

>   ~P v L
>   ~L v P   .

MORE COMPLEX COMPOUNDS

Compound sentences can have more than just two constituents. We have already seen longer disjunctions and conditionals.

>   Al or Bill or Charlie will win the election.   A v B v C
>   If Al wins then either Dave or Ed will be
>   elected treasurer.   ~A v D v E
>   If Al is elected, then if Dave is elected,
>   then Frank will be the membership chairman.   ~A v ~D v F

Conditional and disjunctive sentences that contain conjunctions pose a more difficult problem.

>   If Al and Dave are both elected, then Frank
>   will be the membership chairman.

We can see that this has the same meaning as the last statement above, so we can represent it in the same way.

$$\sim A \ v \sim D \ v \ F$$

For now we will settle on this as the general recipe for conditionals with conjunctive antecedents.

    If A and B, then C $\sim A \ v \sim B \ v \ C.$

 When a conditional has a conjunctive consequent, for example

    If Al wins, then Dave will be elected treasurer and
    Frank will be the membership chairman

it conveys the same information as two conditionals. Thus we use two separate statements

    $\sim A \ v \ D$
    $\sim A \ v \ F$

to represent it. In general

    If A, then B and C $\sim A \ v \ B$
              $\sim A \ v \ C$

 A disjunction containing a conjunctive statement must also be represented by two separate statements.

    Al will win or else George and Harvey will both
    be disappointed

     $A \ v \ G$
     $A \ v \ H$

In general

    A or both B and C $A \ v \ B$
             $A \ v \ C$

 In Chapter Four we will introduce some more direct ways of representing these types of compound statement.

     You should now do Exercises 3B and 3C in the text,
     complete the reading of Chapter Three, and then do
     3c-3e in this study guide and the remaining exer-
     cises in Chapter Three of the text.

Exercise 3c

Use " v " and "~" to symbolize the statements. In some cases you must write more than one statement to adequately represent these.

1. If there are ostriches in Africa, then a very large frying pan will be useful at breakfast there.

2. If Tom doesn't run very fast, collecting ostrich eggs will be very hazardous for him.

3. If there are ostriches in Africa, then we will make sure to take some photographs and we will tell you what an ostrich-egg omlet is like.

4.   Ostriches live in Africa, and rheas are South American.

5.   The ostriches run fast if they see a lion.

6.   If a zebra smells a lion, then the zebras and ostriches run and the lion is not successful.

7.   If the flightless birds of Africa and Australia have a common ancestor, then either Africa and Australia were once much closer together or their nearest common ancestor had the ability to fly.

8.   If the flightless birds of Africa and Australia have no common ancestor or their nearest common ancestor had the ability to fly, then they represent an astonishing case of convergent evolution.

9.   If we don't travel much in Africa, we won't see both ostriches and hippos.

10.   I want to see the lions, but today is the day for beginning our Nile excursion.

11.   We'll see the lions only if we miss the Nile.

12.   Although the herds of game animals are impressive, there is no finer sight than a pride of lions.

13.   If the lions leave their kill, then if the hyenas don't move in first, the vultures clean it up.

14.   We won't see both lions and tigers, but if we stay next week we can see the gnus migrating.

15.   We'll visit Africa if and only if we don't visit Europe.

16.   Neither Africa nor Europe was in my budget last year.

Exercise 3d

Symbolize and show valid.

1.   Either they won't lower interest rates or they won't raise taxes. This is because if they lower interest rates, then there will be no federal revenue problem, and they will raise taxes only if there is a federal revenue problem. (L# Lower interest, R# Raise taxes, F# There will be a federal revenue problem)

2.   If they lower taxes, then if they increase the money supply, then there will be inflation. If there is inflation, the elderly will have a rough time. Thus if they increase the money supply, the elderly will have a rough time, since they will be lowering taxes. (L# Lower taxes, M# Increase money, I# Inflation, R# Elderly have a rough time)

3.   The economy is going to be in big trouble, because it cannot tolerate a drastic drop in the stock market, but there will be one. (T# Economy in big trouble, D# There is a drastic drop in the stock market)

4.   The President will be re-elected only if the economy improves. The economy will improve only if foreign nations cooperate. Thus the President will not be re-elected, because foreign nations will not cooperate. (R# The President is re-elected, E# The economy improves, F# Foreign nations cooperate)

5.   If inflation increases, the elderly will be in financial difficulty. If taxes increase, young adults will be in financial difficulty. If young adults

25

and the elderly are both in financial difficulty, the President will not be re-elected. Thus if the President is to be re-elected, inflation must not increase or taxes must not increase. (I# Inflation increases, E# Elderly in difficulty, T# Taxes increase, Y# Young adults in difficulty, R# The President is re-elected)

Exercise 3e

1. If the Plasmodium parasite is found in all victims of malaria, but not in other people, then it is the source of the disease. If the Plasmodium parasite is found in the Anopheles mosquito and it is the source of the disease, then we should eradicate the Anopheles. So we should eradicate Anopheles, since Plasmodium is found in all victims of malaria, in the Anopheles mosquito, but not in people who do not have malaria.

2. Only a hugh financial commitment will annihilate the mosquito if it is native to the country. Such a commitment will not be made. So we will not annihilate the mosquito if it is native.

3. The rivers will be full only if the monsoon rains are strong. If the rivers are not full, the mosquito will breed more readily than in recent years, and if that happens, many will die of malaria. On the other hand, if the monsoon rains are strong, there will be extensive flood damage. So either there will be extensive flood damage or there will be many who die of malaria.

4. If we control the mosquito, we will use one insecticide or many. If we use just one the mosquito will become resistant and if it becomes resistant we will lose our ability to control it. But if we use many, we don't know what effect that will have on the wildlife. So if we control the mosquito, we will have to live with uncertainity about the wildlife or with an eventual inability to control the mosquito.

5. To eradicate the Anopheles mosquito we must exert strict control over people's movements. But strict control requires military strength and a form of government abhorrent to our people. Without a political revolution, we cannot establish such military strength and we cannot establish such a form of government. Thus eradicating the Anapheles mosquito will require a political revolution.

6. If the mosquito is foreign to the country then if it does not have suitable habitat it will perish. If we drain the swamps, then there will not be suitable habitat for a foreign mosquito. So if we drain the swamps and the mosquito does not perish, it is not foreign.

3a.   1. **1.** A v ~B
        2. B
        3. A   1,2 SC

     3. **1.** A v ~C
        2. C v ~D
        3. ~A
        4. ~C   1,3 SC
        5. ~D   2,4 SC
        Refutes "D".

     5. 1. ~A v B v C
        2. A
        3. ~C
        4. B v C   1,2 SC
        5. B   3,4 SC

     7. 1. A v B v C
        2. ~A
        3. B v C   1,2 SC
        NC. Cannot establish or refute "B".

     9. 1. ~B
        2. B v ~A
        3. B v C
        4. A v ~C v D
        5. ~A   1,2 SC
        6. C   1,3 SC
        7. ~C v D   4,5 SC
        8. D   6,7 SC

3b. Keep in mind that for most of these there are several correct ways to use the inference rules to derive the conclusion.

     1. **1.** A v B
        2. ~C v ~A
        3. ~E v C
        4. ~E v ~A   2,3 CC
        5. ~E v B   1,4 CC

     3. 1. ~A v B
        2. ~A v C
        3. ~B v ~C
        4. ~A v ~C   1,3 CC
        5. ~A v ~A   2,4 CC
        6. ~A   5 Rep.

     5. 1. ~A v B v C
        2. ~B
        3. ~A v C v B 1 Comm
        4. ~A v C   2,3 SC

     7. 1. ~A v B
        2. ~C v D
        3. A v C
        4. C v B   1,3 CC
        5. B v D   2,4 CC

     9. 1. ~A v B
        2. ~B v C
        3. ~B v D
        4. ~A v B v B 1 Rep.
        5. ~A v B v C 2,4 CC
        6. ~A v C v B 5 Comm
        7. ~A v C v D 3,6 CC

     2. 1. A
        2. ~C v B
        3. ~A v C v D
        4. C v D   1,3 SC
        5. B v D   2,4 CC

     4. 1. ~A v C v D
        2. A
        3. C v D   1,2 SC
        4. D v C   2,4 CC

     6. 1. A v B v C
        2. ~C
        3. A v B   1,2 SC
        4. B v A   3 Comm
        5. B v ~~A   4 DN

     8. 1. F v A
        2. F v C
        3. ~C v ~A
        4. F v ~A   2,3 CC
        5. F v F   1,4 CC
        6. F   5 Rep.

    10. 1. A v B v C
        2. ~C v D
        3. ~B v D
        4. A v B v D   1,2 CC
        5. A v D v B   4 Comm
        6. A v D v D   3,5 CC
        7. A v D   6 Rep.

```
3c.   1.  ~O v U
      2.  ~~R v H
      3.  ~O v P
          ~O v T
      4.  O
          R
      5.  ~L v R
      6.  ~S v Z
          ~S v O
          ~S v ~L
      7.  ~B v C v F
      8.  ~~B v E
          ~F v E
      9.  ~~T v ~O v ~H
     10.  L
          N
     11.  ~L v M
     12.  H
          ~F
     13.  ~L v ~~H v V
     14.  ~L v ~T
          ~S v G
     15.  ~A v ~E
          ~~E v A
     16.  ~A
          ~E

3d.   1.  1.  ~L v ~F
          2.  ~R v F
          3.  ~L v ~R          1,2 CC

      2.  1.  ~L v ~M v I
          2.  ~I v R
          3.  L
          4.  ~M v I           1,3 SC
          5.  ~M v R           2,4 CC

      3.  1.  ~D v T
          2.  D
          3.  T                1,2 SC

      4.  1.  ~R v E
          2.  ~E v F
          3.  ~F
          4.  ~E               1,3 SC
          5.  ~R               1,4 SC

      5.  1.  ~I v E
          2.  ~T v Y
          3.  ~Y v ~E v ~R
          4.  ~T v ~E v ~R     2,3 CC
          5.  ~E v ~T v ~R     4 Comm
          6.  ~I v ~T v ~R     1,5 CC
          7.  ~R v ~I v ~T     6 Comm
```

```
3e.   1.  1.  ~V v ~~O v S
          2.  ~A v ~S v E
          3.  V
          4.  A
          5.  ~O
          6.  ~~O v S          1,3 SC
          7.  S                5,6 SC
          8.  ~S v E           2,4 SC
          9.  E                7,8 SC

      2.  1.  ~N v ~A v H
          2.  ~H
          3.  ~N v ~A          1,2 SC

      3.  1.  ~R v S
          2.  ~~R v B
          3.  ~B v D
          4.  ~S v E
          5.  S v B            1,2 CC
          6.  S v D            3,5 CC
          7.  E v D            4,6 CC

      4.  1.  ~C v O v M
          2.  ~O v R
          3.  ~R v L
          4.  ~M v ~K
          5.  ~C v O v ~K      1,4 CC
          6.  ~C v ~K v O      5 Comm
          7.  ~C v ~K v R      2,6 CC
          8.  ~C v ~K v L      3,7 CC

      5.  1.  ~E v C
          2.  ~C v M
          3.  ~C v G
          4.  ~M v ~G v R
          5.  ~E v M           1,2 CC
          6.  ~E v ~G v R      4,5 CC
          7.  ~E v G           1,3 CC
          8.  ~G v ~E v R      6 Comm
          9.  ~E v ~E v R      7,8 CC
         10.  ~E v R           9 Rep

      6.  1.  ~F v ~~H v P
          2.  ~D v ~F v ~H
          3.  ~F v P v ~~H          1 Comm
          4.  ~D v ~F v ~F v P      2,3 CC
          5.  ~D v ~F v P          4 Rep
          6.  ~D v P v ~F          5 Comm
          7.  ~D v ~~P v ~F        6 DN
```

CHAPTER FOUR

In the text, read the opening of Chapter Four and
the section "Truth Tables and Variables." Then
read the following three sections of this study
guide.

STATEMENT LOGIC: THE COMPLETE SYSTEM

     In Chapter Four we extend the system of Chapter Three so that it is adequate
to deal with more arguments involving compound statements. In doing so, we will
introduce symbols that make the representation of some English compounds simpler.
In addition, the precise character of these statement connectives (they are
"truth-functional") will be made clearer.

STATEMENT PATTERNS

     In developing the logic of compound statements, we will often need to talk
about all statements, all disjunctions, all disjunctions in which both disjuncts
are the same statement, etc.

For example

          (I)   If the right disjunct of a disjunction is the   .
                negation of the left disjunct, then the disjunction
                must be true.

          (II) If an argument has two premises and one is a disjunction
                and the other is the negation of the right disjunct,
                and if the conclusion is the same as the left disjunct
                of the disjunctive premise, then the argument is valid.

(I) and (II) are relatively simple examples of the sort of thing we will want to
say, but they are already quite cumbersome. To make our discussions easier, it
will be useful to use symbols and to talk about all statements (or arguments)
of a certain form. Thus we might re-write (I) and (II) .

(I')   All statements with the pattern

$$\underline{\hspace{3em}} \text{ v } \sim \underline{\hspace{3em}}$$

must be true

(II')   All arguments with the pattern

$$\frac{\underline{\hspace{2em}} \text{ v } \ldots}{\begin{array}{c} \sim \ldots \\ \hline \underline{\hspace{2em}} \end{array}}$$

are valid.

We can understand these presentations of statement and argument forms as allowing us to put statements in the blanks, with the same statement in the same type blank.

   In fact, it is even easier to read, as well as more convenient typographically, if we use letters instead of blanks for this.   Thus

(I")   All statements with the pattern "p v ~p" are true

(II")   All arguments with the pattern

$$\frac{\begin{array}{c} p \text{ v } q \\ \sim q \end{array}}{p}$$

are valid.

Whenever we substitute statements (or capital letters abbreviating statements) we get a particular example of the pattern being discussed. Thus (I) tells us that "A v ~A", "(B v A) v ~(B v A)", "[(B v C) v ~A] v ~[(B v C) v ~A]","~A v ~~A", etc. are all true. Each is of the indicated pattern. (II") tells us that an infinite number of instances of simple cancellation are valid. For example,

$$\frac{\begin{array}{c} A \text{ v } B \\ \sim B \end{array}}{A} \qquad \frac{\begin{array}{c} (A \text{ v } B) \text{ v } \sim C \\ \sim\sim C \end{array}}{A \text{ v } B} \qquad \frac{\begin{array}{c} A \text{ v } (C \text{ v } D) \\ \sim(C \text{ v } D) \end{array}}{A}$$

   Symbolic expressions with "p", "q", "r", and "s" will be called statement patterns. Particular sentences are instances of statement patterns.   Thus the sentence

(S)   A v ~(B v C)

is an instance of the statement patterns

(a)   p
(b)   p v q
(c)   p v ~q
(d)   p v ~(q v r)

because

(a)   Every statement is an instance of "p" (which is, in effect, just a single blank for putting in statements)
(b)   Every disjunction is an instance of "p v q" (and (S) is a disjunction)
(c)   Every disjunction with a negated right disjunct is an instance of "p v ~q"
(d)   Every disjunction that has a negated disjunction for its right disjunct

is an instance of "p v ~(q v r)".

Recognizing the forms a statement has in one of the most important steps in determining what valid inferences it can be a part of.

For each of the sentences on the left, list the forms (on the right) of which it is an instance.

1. A v B
2. A v ~B
3. A **v** (B v C)
4. ~(B v C) v A
5. ~(A v B) v C
6. ~A
7. ~(A v B)
8. ~[(A v B) v C]
9. ~(~A v B)
10. ~[(~A v B) v C]

a. p
b. q
c. ~p
d. p v q
e. p v ~q
f. ~p v q
g. p v (q v r)
h. (p v q) v r
i. ~(p v q)
j. ~(p v q) v r

k. ~[(p v q) v r]
l. ~(~p v q)
m. ~[(~p v q) v r]

Now read the sections of the text entitled "Tautologies",
"New Connectives" and "Parentheses and the Main Connective."
Then read the next section of the study guide.

TRUTH-FUNCTIONAL COMPOUNDS

For many compound statements, the truth-value of the statement as a whole can be determined whenever we know the truth-value of the constituent statements.

Roses are red and violets are blue.

This compound statement has two constituent statements

Roses are red.
Violets are blue.

The compound statement is true if each of the constituent statements is true, and if one or both of the constituents is false, the compound is false.

If the truth-value of a compound statement depends upon the truth-value of the constituent statements, the compound is truth-functional. We can use a table to indicate this relationship. We list all possible combinations of truth-values, and indicate the truth value of the compound in each case.

Roses are red.	Violets are blue	Roses are red and violets are blue
T	T	T
T	F	F
F	T	F
F	F	F

The study of truth-functional compounds will give us valuable insight into why inferences of some forms are valid. Our symbols for making compound statements will represent different truth-functional relationships. A dot symbol will be used between statements to create a compound statement, and the truth-value of the compound will depend upon the truth-values of the constituents in the way indicated in this table.

p	q	p · q
T	T	T
T	F	F
F	T	F
F	F	F

Since the English connective "and" is used in compounds that conform to this table, we can use "·" to represent "and".

Although the words "but" and "and" are different in their suggestions, "but" is also a connective that is used in compounds that conform to the table for "·". "Roses are red but violets are blue" has the same truth-conditions as "Roses are red and violets are blue," even though the sentences may differ in other respects. Thus "·" may be used to represent "but" and any other compound statements with appropriate truth-conditions.

Negation is also truth-functional, and can be defined by the table

p	~p
T	F
F	T

And we will now use the symbol for disjunction to represent truth-functional compounds of the following type.

p	q	p v q
T	T	T
T	F	T
F	T	T
F	F	F

This corresponds to the <u>inclusive</u> sense of "or". "In 1990, we'll have energy shortages or food shortages (maybe both)." (This contrasts with a statement like "You'll eat your beans or you'll be punished" which may use "or" in the <u>exclusive</u> sense, to exclude the case in which both disjuncts are true.)

Since " · ", "v" and "~" are truth-functional statement connectives, we can always determine the truth-vlaue of a statement involving them if we know the truth-values of the constituent statements.

So if "A" and "B" represent true statements and C represents a false statement, we can determine the truth-value of compounds involving them as indicated in this example.

$$(A \ v \ C) \cdot (B \cdot \sim C)$$

Beginning with the truth-assignments made to the basic constituents, we can determine the truth-value of progressivley longer statements until the truth-value of the entire compound is known.

<u>Exercise 4b</u>

Suppose we know that "A" and "B" represent true statements, and "C" and "D"

32

represent false statements. What is the truth-value of each of these compound statements?

1.   A · B
2.   A · C
3.   A · ~C
4.   A v C
5.   C v D
6.   C v ~D
7.   ~(A · B)
8.   ~(C · D)
9.   ~(A · D)
10. ~(~A · B)
11. A v (B · C)
12. C v (A · B)
13. ~C · (A v D)
14. ~C · ~(A · D)
15. ~[D · ~(C · A)]

Proceed to the next section of the study guide.

TAUTOLOGIES AND CONTRADICTIONS

     Some statement patterns have only true instances. Given any substitution of statements (no matter what truth-values those statements have) the compound statement must be true.   A disjunction with the pattern "[(p · q) v (p · ~q)] v ~p" will always be true no matter what truth-values the statements in positions p and q have. We can verify this by considering all possible assignments to p and q.

P	q	[(p · q) v (p · ~q)] v ~p				
T	T	T T T	T	T T FT	T FT
T	F	T F F	T	T T TF	T FT
F	T	F F T	F	F F FT	T TF
F	F	F F F	F	F F TF	T TF

Thus all statements of this form must be true.   So

        [(A · B) v (A · ~B)] v ~A
        {[(A · B) · C] v [(A · B) · ~C]} v ~(A · B)
        [(~C · D) v (~C · ~D)] v ~~C

are all true. Statement forms with only true instances are tautologies.

     Similarly, if all statements with a certain pattern are false, that statement pattern is a contradiction.

p	p · ~p		
T	T F FT
F	F F TF

No matter what is in the position held by "p", we will have a false statement.

        A · ~A
        ~B · ~~B
        (A · C) · ~(A · C)

must all be false no matter what the truth-values of "A", "~B" and "A · C" are.

33

If a statement form has both true and false instances, it is <u>contingent</u>.

p	q	p v q
T	T	T
T	F	T
F	T	T
F	F	F

There is at least one true row, and at least one false row.

Exercise 4c

Which of the following forms are <u>tautologies</u>, which are contradictions, and which are <u>contingent</u>?

1. (p v q) v ~p
2. p · q
3. (~p · q) · (p v ~q)
4. p · (q v r)
5. ~p v (~q · ~r)
6. [p · (q v r)] v [~p v (~q · ~r)]
7. ~(p v ~p)
8. (p v ~p) v (p · q)
9. (p v ~p) · (p · ~p)
10. ~[(p · q) · (~p v ~q)]

Continue to the next section of the study guide.

CONDITIONALS AND BICONDITIONALS

We can represent conditionals more directly than we did in Chapter Three by using " ⊃ ", defined by the following table.

P	q	p ⊃ q
T	T	T
T	F	F
F	T	T
F	F	T

Statements of this form have the same truth-conditions as statements of the form "~p v q", the representation of conditional employed in Chapter Three. This represents the common element in all conditionals. Any statement of the form "p ⊃ q" definitely rules out the possibility that p is true and q is false. Thus "p ⊃ q" is false on that row of the table. (Note that this is all that is clearly ruled out.)

Occasionally we will want to represent statements like "we will avoid an energy shortage if and only if we undertake strict conservation measures now." - "A if and only if C". We will use the symbol " ≡ ", defined as:

p	q	p ≡ q
T	T	T
T	F	F
F	T	F
F	F	T

Thus we represent the statement as "A ≡ C".

34

Exercise 4d

Let "A" and "B" stand for true statements, "C" and "D" for false statements. The truth-value of "E" will be left unknown. Determine the truth-value of each of these compounds if possible.

1. A ⊃ B
2. A ⊃ C
3. C ⊃ A
4. C ⊃ (D v B)
5. ~D ⊃ C
6. A ⊃ (B · C)
7. (A · C) ⊃ B
8. (A · ~C) ⊃ B

9. ~(A · C) ⊃ D
10. A ≡ B
11. ~(A ≡ B)
12. ~(A ≡ C)
13. A ≡ (E v B)
14. E ⊃ A
15. C ⊃ E

Exercise 4e

Which are <u>tautologies</u>, which <u>contradictions</u>, and which <u>contingent</u>?

1. p ⊃ p
2. (p · q) ⊃ p
3. p ≡ ~~p
4. p ⊃ ~p
5. p ⊃ (p v q)
6. (p · q) ⊃ (q · p)

7. (p v q) ⊃ p
8. p ⊃ (p v q)
9. (p v ~p) ⊃ (p · ~p)
10. (p · q) ⊃ ~(~p v ~q)
11. [(p · q) · r] ≡ [p · (q · r)]
12. [p · (q v r)] ≡ [(p · q) v r]

Exercise 4f

Using the new connectives " · ", " ⊃ " and " ≡ ", symbolize the sentences of Exercise 3c.

> Now read the section in the text "Testing validity by Truth-table." Then read the next section of the study guide.

TESTING VALIDITY BY TRUTH TABLE

An argument is valid if and only if there is no way for its premises to be true and its conclusion false. A conditional is a tautology if and only if there is no way for its antecedent to be true and its consequent false. (Thus the conditional does not come out false on any truth-assignment.) So each valid argument corresponds to a tautologous conditional in which the premises of the argument are conjoined to form the antecedent of the conditional and the conclusion of the argument is the consequent of the conditional.

Consider these two argument forms

(A)	p ⊃ q	(B)	p ⊃ q
	p		q
	q		p

By forming the corresponding conditionals we can test these for validity.

p	q			[(p ⊃ q) · p] ⊃ q		
T	T			T T T T T	T T	
T	F			T F F F T	T F	
F	T			F T T F F	T T	
F	F			F T F F F	T F	

Since this conditional is true in every case, it is a tautology. Since the corresponding conditional is a tautology, (A) is valid.

p	q			[(p ⊃ q) · q] ⊃ p		
T	T			T T T T T T	T	
T	F			T F F F F T	T	
F	T			F T T T T F	F	
F	F			F T F F F T	F	

Since this is not a tautology, argument (B) is not valid. There is a case in which its premises are true and its conclusion is false. (The third row of the table is the invalidating case. "p ⊃ q" and "q" are true, but "p" is false.)

Exercise 4g

Determine whether these argument forms are valid or invalid.

1. p v q
    p   ~q

2. p ⊃ q
    ~q   ~p

3. p · q   p

4. p   p v q

5. (p · q) ⊃ r
    p   q ⊃ r

6. (p v q) ⊃ r   p ⊃ r

7. p
    p ⊃ (q · r)   r

8. p ⊃ ~q
    q   ~p

9. p ≡ q
    q   p

10. p ≡ (q · r)
    q   r ⊃ ~p

You can now try Exercise 4A in the text. The section "Truth Table Shortcut" describes a more convenient method for testing for validity. Do Exercises 4g and 4A again, using this technique. Now read the section "New Rules" in the text, and do Exercises 4B and 4C. Then read the next section of the study guide.

SOME NEW RULES

To allow the use of the new connectives in derivations, we must add some rules involving them.

Exercise 4h

Let us add the following group of new rules to the rules already available to us. (SC, CC, Comm, DN, Rep)

Simp $\dfrac{A \cdot B}{A}$ $\dfrac{A \cdot B}{B}$

36

	Conj	A	CJ	~A v B
		B		A · C
		A · B		B · C

	MP	A ⊃ B	MT	A ⊃ B
		A		~B
		B		~A

Using these rules, do a derivation refuting or establishing the conclusion in each case.

1. A ⊃ (B · C)
    A v D   D?
    ~(B · C)

2. (A · B) ⊃ C
    A · D   C?
    D ⊃ B

3. ~A v ~C
    A · B   D?
    (~C · B) ⊃ ~D

4. A v (B · C)
    ~A · (B ⊃ D)   D?

5. (A · B) ⊃ C
    (D · E) ⊃ ~C
    D ⊃ E   A · B?
    D

6. A ⊃ (D v C)
    B ⊃ (~C · E)
    ~A v B   D · E?
    A

Read the rest of Chapter Four, then
proceed to the next section of the
study guide.

CONDITIONAL PROOF

The most important rule of this chapter is the Rule of Conditional Proof. It captures a form of inference that is at the core of many of the derivations that one commonly sees. In a conditional proof, we explore the consequences of an assumption and conclude with a conditional that formulates the results of this exploration.

The best way to see how conditional proof works is to consider an example of its use. (Our discussion is deliberately detailed in order to make the character of the derivation clear.) Consider the following argument:

> If we buy a stereo, we must cut down on small purchases
> or our financial plans will be ruined. If we buy more
> records, we will not be cutting down on small purchases.
> But if we buy a stereo, we will buy more records. So
> if we buy a stereo, our financial plans will be ruined.

The conclusion is a conditional. Although it is fairly obvious that the argument is valid, if called upon to establish this we could proceed in the following way (lines 4-9).

1. If we buy a stereo, we must cut   S ⊃ (C v R)   (premise)
    down on small purchases or our
    financial plans will be ruined.

2. If we buy more records, we will   M ⊃ ~C   (premise)
    not be cutting down on small
    purchases.

3.	If we buy a stereo, we will buy more records.	S ⊃ M	(premise)
*4.	Suppose we buy a stereo.	<u>Suppose</u> S	
*5.	Then we must cut down on small purchases or our financial plans will be ruined.	C v R	1,4 MP
*6.	But we will also buy more records.	M	3,4 MP
*7.	Then we will not be cutting down.	~C	2,6 MP
*8.	Then our financial plans will be ruined.	R	5,7 SC
9.	So if we buy a stereo, our financial plans will be ruined.	S ⊃ R	

The supposition of step 4 (that we buy a stereo) leads to the result stated in step 8 (that our financial plans will be ruined). Thus we conclude with the conditional of step 9 (that if we buy a stereo, our financial plans will be ruined).

We need to supplement our formal system with rules that will allow steps like 4 and 9 of the above derivation. We must be allowed to make assumptions, and explore the consequences of those assumptions, and draw conditional conclusions on that basis. So we now introduce two new rules. One (ACP) allows the introduction of an assumption and the other (RCP) allows us to state the conditional conclusion that is established.

ACP (Assumption for Conditional Proof) allows us to write an assumption as a line of a derivation. We must mark that line with an asterisk to indicate that it is an assumption, and we must also mark an asterisk on the lines that depend upon the assumption (in the way that lines 5-8 depend upon line 4 in the derivation given above). They are the exploration of the consequences of the assumption.

RCP (the Rule of Conditional Proof) allows us to explicitly state the result that we have established by our explorations. Since step 4 leads to step 8, the conditional that has the formula of 4 ("S") as its antecedent and the formula of 8 as its consequent ("R") must be true. (In other words, since the supposition that we buy a stereo implies that our financial plans are ruined, the conditional "if we buy a stereo, then our financial plans will be ruined" must be true.) We may write this contidional ("S ⊃ R") on line 9 without an asterisk. It is justified by lines 4-8, our exploration of the consequences of 4.

The completed derivation will look like this.

1.	S ⊃ (C v R)	
2.	M ⊃ ~C	
3.	S ⊃ M	
*4.	S	ACP
*5.	C v R	1,4 MP
*6.	M	3,4 MP
*7.	~ C	2,6 MP
*8.	R	5,7 SC
9.	S ⊃ R	4-8 RCP

<u>Strategy Tips</u>

Conditional proof is the most common means employed in deriving conditionals. Expect to use it often.

ACP allows any formula to be introduced as a line of proof provided that the line and all lines depending on it are marked with an asterisk. However, no derivation can end with a line marked by an asterisk, and RCP is the only rule that employs asterisked lines to derive unasterisked lines. (So ACP will be useful only when its use enables one to derive a helpful conditional by RCP.)

Even when my conclusion is not a conditional, it may be helpful to derive a conditional.

```
 1.   [A ⊃ (B · C)] ⊃ D
 2.   A ⊃ B                                    D?
 3.   A ⊃ C
*4.   A                              ACP
*5.   B                              2,4 MP
*6.   C                              3,4 MP
*7.   B · C                          5,6 Conj.
 8.   A ⊃ (B · C)                    4-7 RCP
 9.   D                              1,8 MP
```

This derivation does not conclude with a conditional, but it does use conditional proof to establish a useful conditional (in line 8).

ACP and RCP allow us to establish a conclusion indirectly, by assuming its denial. If I wish to establish C, I may assume ~C(using ACP) and then derive C(as an asterisked line). I can then use RCP to derive "~ C ⊃ C", which is equivalent to C.

```
  1.   B ⊃ [~S ⊃ (D v N)]
  2.   B · ~ D
  3.   ~N
  4.   B                             2 Simp
  5.   ~ D                           2 Simp
  6.   ~ S ⊃ (D v N)                 1-4 MP
 *7.   ~ S                           ACP
 *8.   D v N                         6,7 MP
 *9.   N                             5,8 SC
*10.   N · ~ N                       3,9 Conj.
*11.   S                             10 Contr
 12.   ~ S ⊃ S                       7-11 RCP
 13.   ~~ S v S                      12 DMI
 14.   S v S                         13 DN
 15.   S                             14 REP
```

There is a complete list of rules on the following page. You should now do the remaining exercises of Chapter Four in the text and in the study guide. You will probably find their order of difficulty to be: 4D, 4E, 4i, 4j, 4F, 4k.

THE COMPLETE SYSTEM

<u>SC</u> $\dfrac{A \lor B,\ \sim A}{B}$ $\dfrac{A \lor B,\ \sim B}{A}$ <u>MP</u> $\dfrac{A \supset B,\ A}{B}$ <u>CJ</u> $\dfrac{\sim A \lor B,\ A \cdot C}{B \cdot C}$

  $\dfrac{\sim A \lor B,\ A}{B}$ $\dfrac{A \lor \sim B,\ B}{A}$ <u>HS</u> $\dfrac{A \supset B,\ B \supset C}{A \supset C}$ <u>MT</u> $\dfrac{A \supset B,\ \sim B}{\sim A}$

<u>CC</u> $\dfrac{A \lor B,\ \sim B \lor C}{A \lor C}$ $\dfrac{A \lor B,\ C \lor \sim B}{A \lor C}$ <u>DD</u> $\dfrac{\sim A \lor \sim B,\ C \supset A,\ D \supset B}{\sim C \lor \sim D}$ <u>CD</u> $\dfrac{A \lor B,\ A \supset C,\ B \supset D}{C \lor D}$

<u>Simp</u> $\dfrac{A \cdot B}{A}$ $\dfrac{A \cdot B}{B}$ <u>Add</u> $\dfrac{A}{A \lor B}$ <u>Contr</u> $\dfrac{A \cdot \sim A}{B}$

<u>Conj</u> $\dfrac{A,\ B}{A \cdot B}$

Equivalence (two-way interchange) rules

<u>Comm</u> $\dfrac{A \lor B}{B \lor A}$ $\dfrac{A \cdot B}{B \cdot A}$ $\dfrac{A \equiv B}{B \equiv A}$ <u>Exp</u> $\dfrac{A \supset (B \supset C)}{(A \cdot B) \supset C}$

<u>Rep</u> $\dfrac{A \lor A}{A}$ $\dfrac{A \cdot A}{A}$ <u>Dist</u> $\dfrac{A \cdot (B \lor C)}{(A \cdot B) \lor (A \cdot C)}$

<u>DeM</u> $\dfrac{\sim(A \lor B)}{\sim A \cdot \sim B}$ $\dfrac{\sim(A \cdot B)}{\sim A \lor \sim B}$ <u>DN</u> $\dfrac{A}{\sim\sim A}$

<u>DMI</u> $\dfrac{A \supset B}{\sim A \lor B}$ <u>DME</u> $\dfrac{A \equiv B}{(A \supset B) \cdot (B \supset A)}$

<u>Transp</u> $\dfrac{A \supset B}{\sim B \supset \sim A}$ <u>Comp</u> $\dfrac{A \equiv B}{\sim A \equiv \sim B}$

<u>Assoc</u> $\dfrac{(A \cdot B) \cdot C}{A \cdot (B \cdot C)}$ $\dfrac{(A \lor B) \lor C}{A \lor (B \lor C)}$ <u>Abs</u> $\dfrac{A \supset B}{A \supset (A \cdot B)}$

Conditional Proof (RCP and ACP)

A statement "A" is assumed (ACP)
and each line depending on it
receives an *. If "B" appears
as a subsequent line, "A ⊃ B"
may be written as the next line,
without an * (RCP).

```
          .       .
          .       .
          .       .
*n.       A              ACP
          .       .
          .       .
          .       .
*m.       B
m+1.      A ⊃ B          n-m, RCP
          .       .
          .       .
          .       .
```

Do a derivation to establish or refute the suggested conclusion.

1. A ⊃ (D ⊃ C)
    B ⊃ ~C   A ⊃ ~D?
    B

2. A ⊃ ~D
    ~D ⊃ ~C   A ⊃ B?
    B v C

3. (A v B) ⊃ C
    ~E   A?
    ~C v E

4. ~A v B
    A ⊃ C   D v ~A?
    (B · C) ⊃ D

5. C ⊃ ~(E · A)
    D ⊃ A   G?
    B ⊃ E
    G ⊃ (D · B)
    C

6. D ⊃ A
    D ⊃ (E · F)   ~C ⊃ (A · F)?
    D v (B · C)

7. D ⊃ A
    ~D ⊃ ~B   A?
    ~A ⊃ (C v B)
    ~C

8. (B v C) ⊃ (D · E)
    (D v ~E) ⊃ B   D v E?

9. ~D ⊃ ~E
    (D · ~A) ⊃ F   (A v C) v F?
    E v (A v C)

10. D
    (D · C) ⊃ ~G
    (D · ~C) ⊃ B   G?
    B ⊃ ~G

11. A ≡ B
    ~(B · C)   A?
    C

12. A ⊃ (B · C)
    B ⊃ D   A ≡ B?
    A v ~D

Exercise 4i

Symbolize and prove valid.

1. If the Kiwi's large egg size is an evolutionary development from a bird of similar size, then large egg size must have an adaptive value. If it is not an evolutionary development from a bird of similar size, then the Kiwi must have had some very large ancestors. So the Kiwi must have had some very large ancestors, since large egg size has no adaptive value.

2. If the flightless birds of Africa and Australia have a common ancestor, then either Africa and Australia were once much closer together or the nearest common ancestor of these birds had the ability to fly. But if they have no common ancestor or the nearest common ancestor had the ability to fly, then this is an astonishing case of convergent evolution. So either this is an astonishing case of convergent evolution, or else Africa and Australia were once much closer together.

3. Bright color in male birds must be a result of natural selection or sexual selection. If it is a result of natural selection, it must help them in adapting to their environment. If female birds are color blind, it cannot be a result of sexual selection. So if female birds are color blind, then bright color in male birds must help them in adapting to their environment.

4. If female birds are color blind, then bright color in males is not a result of sexual selection. But if it is not a result of sexual selection then if it does not camouflage them or help them chase away predators, then it must help in establishing territory. It can help in establishing territory only if male birds are not color blind. Bright color does not camouflage male birds, and it does not help them chase away predators. So if female birds are color blind, male birds are not color blind.

5. If female birds are color blind, then male birds are not color blind. But either both are color blind or else neither is. So female birds are not color blind.

Exercise 4k

Symbolize and prove valid.

1. We can reduce energy consumption by autos only if we increase the efficiency of engines or reduce the number of miles driven. We cannot reduce the number of miles driven, so we cannot reduce energy consumption by autos without increasing the efficiency of engines.

2. We will not significantly reduce energy consumption by autos unless we increase their efficiency under the most common driving conditions. To increase efficiency under the most common driving conditions, we must use an engine that is efficient at low power. Since we will have to significantly reduce energy consumption if we are to avoid economic disaster, if we are to avoid economic disaster we must use an engine that is efficient at low power.

3. If cars with high emissions are most heavily taxed, then they will become comparatively expensive. If so, people will not buy them. If people don't buy them, they will be taken off the market. Thus if cars with high emissions are most heavily taxed, they will be taken off the market.

4. If emissions controls can be made to last the life of a car, then the internal combustion engine will be the cheapest to maintain and among the lowest in emissions. If it is among the lowest in emissions, it will be the dominant engine if it is also cheap to maintain. So if the emission controls can be made to last the life of the car, the internal combustion engine will be dominant.

5. If automobiles produce pollution that is costly to deal with, then if they are not to be a burden on society, they will be taxed more heavily or regulated. Regulation will be either stringent or lenient. If it is stringent, automobiles will be difficult to buy. If it is lenient, automobiles will be a burden on society anyway. Since automobiles do produce costly pollution, if they are not to be difficult to buy and they are not to be a burden on society, they must be taxed more heavily.

Answers

4a

1. A v B: p, q, p v q.
3. A v (B v C): p, q, p v q, p v (q v r).
5. ~(A v B) v A: p, q, p v q, ~p v q, ~(p v q) v r.
7. ~(A v B): p,q, ~p, ~(p v q).
9. ~(~A v B): p, q, ~p, ~(p v q), ~(~p v q).

4b	4c	4d	4e
1. T	1. Tautology	1. T	1. Tautology
3. T	3. Contradiction	3. T	3. Tautology
5. F	5. Contingent	5. F	5. Contingent
7. F	7. Contradiction	7. T	7. Contingent
9. T	9. Contradiction	9. F	9. Contradiction
11. T		11. F	11. Tautology
13. T		13. T	
15. T		15. T	

4f

1. O ⊃ U
2. ~R ⊃ H
3. O ⊃ (P · T)
4. O · R
5. L ⊃ R
6. S ⊃ [(Z · O) · ~L]
7. B ⊃ (C v F)
8. (~B v F) ⊃ E
9. ~T ⊃ ~(O · H)
10. L · N
11. L ⊃ M
12. H · ~F
13. L ⊃ (~H ⊃ V)
14. ~(L · T) · (S ⊃ G)
15. A ≡ ~E
16. ~(A v E)

4g

1.

p	q	[(p v q) · p] ⊃ ~q	
T	T	T T T T T F FT	Not valid.
T	F		
F	T		
F	F		

3.

p	q	(p · q) ⊃ p	
T	T	T T T T T	Valid.
T	F	T F F T T	
F	T	F F T	
F	F	F F T	

5.

p	q	r	{[(p · q) ⊃ r] · p}⊃ (q ⊃ r)	
T	T	T	T T T	Valid.
T	T	F	T T T F F F T T T F F	
T	F	T	T T T	
T	F	F	T F F T F T T T F T F	
F	T	T	F F T T T	
F	T	F	F F T	
F	F	T	F F T	
F	F	F	F F T	

43

7.

p	q	r	{p · [p ⊃ (q · r)]} ⊃ r	
T	T	T		T T
T	T	F	T F T F T F F	T F
T	F	T		T T
T	F	F	T F T F F F F	T F
F	T	T	F F	T T
F	T	F	F F	T
F	F	T	F F	T T
F	F	F	F F	T

Valid.

9.

p	q	[(p ≡ q) · q] ⊃ p	
T	T		T T
T	F		T T
F	T	F F T F T	T F
F	F	F F	T

Valid.

4h

1.
1. A ⊃ (B · C)
2. A v D
3. ~(B · C)
4. ~A   1, 3 MT
5. D   2, 4 SC

3.
1. ~A v ~C
2. A · B
3. (~C · B) ⊃ ~D
4. A   2, Simp
5. B   2, Simp
6. ~C   1,4 SC
7. ~C · B   5,6 Conj
8. ~D   3,7 MP

    Refutes "D"

5.
1. (A · B) ⊃ C
2. (D · E) ⊃ ~C
3. D ⊃ E
4. D
5. E   3,4 MP
6. D · E   4,5 Conj
7. ~C   2,6 MP
8. ~(A · B)   1,7 MT

    Refutes "A · B"

4i

1.
1.   A ⊃ (D ⊃ C)
2.   B ⊃ ~C
3.   B
4.   ~C   2,3 MP
*5. A   ACP
*6. D ⊃ C   1,5 MP
*7. ~D   4,6 MP
8.   A ⊃ ~D   5-7 RCP

3.
1. (A v B) ⊃ C
2. ~E
3. ~C v E
4. ~C   2,3 SC
5. ~(A v B)   1,4 MT
6. ~A · ~B   5 DEM
7. ~A   6 Simp

    Refutes "A".

5.
1.   C ⊃ ~(E · A)
2.   D ⊃ A
3.   B ⊃ E
4.   G ⊃ (D · B)
5.   C
6.   ~(E · A)   1,5 MP
*7. G   ACP
*8. D · B   4,7 MP
*9. D   8 Simp
*10. B   8 Simp
*11. A   2,9 MP
*12. E   3,10 MP
*13. E · A   11,12 Conj
*14. (E · A) · ~(E · A) 6,13 Conj
*15. ~G   14 Contr.
16. G ⊃ ~G   7-15 RCP
17. ~G v ~G   16 DMI
18. ~G   Rep

     Refutes "G"

7. 1. D ⊃ A
    2. ~D ⊃ ~B
    3. ~A ⊃ (C v B)
    4. ~C
   *5. ~A   ACP
   *6. C v B   3,5 MP
   *7. B   4,7 SC
   *8. ~~B   7, DN
   *9. ~~D   2,8 MT

  *10. D   9 DN
  *11. ~D   1,5 MT
  *12. D · ~D   10,11 Conj
  *13. A   12 Contr.
   14. ~A ⊃ A   5,13 RCP
   15. ~~A v A   14 DMI
   16. A v A   15 DN
   17. A   16 REP

9. 1. ~D ⊃ ~E
    2. (D · ~A) ⊃ F
    3. E v (A v C)
   *4. ~(A v C)   ACP
   *5. E   3,4 SC
   *6. ~~E   5 DN
   *7. ~~D   1,6 MT
   *8. D   7 DN

   *9. ~A · ~C   4 DEM
  *10. ~A   9 Simp
  *11. D · ~A   8,10 Conj
  *12. F   2,11 MP
   13. ~(A v C) ⊃ F   4,12 RCP
   14. ~~(A v C) v F   13 DMI
   15. (A v C) v F   14 DN

11. 1. A ≡ B
     2. ~(B · C)
     3. C
    *4. A   ACP
    *5. (A ⊃ B) · (B ⊃ A)   1 DME
    *6. A ⊃ B   5 Simp
    *7. B   4,6 MP

    *8. B · C   3,7 Conj
    *9. (B · C) · ~(B · C)   8,2 Conj
   *10. ~A   9 Contr
    11. A ⊃ ~A   4,10 RCP
    12. ~A v ~A   11 DMI
    13. ~A   12 REP

4j

1. 1. E ⊃ A
    2. ~E ⊃ L
    3. ~A
    4. ~E   1,3 MT
    5. L   2,4 MP

3. 1. N v S
    2. N ⊃ A
    3. F ⊃ ~S
   *4. F   ACP
   *5. ~S   3,4 MP
   *6. N   1,5 SC
   *7. A   1,6 MP
    8. F ⊃ A   4-7 RCP

5. 1. F ⊃ ~M
    2. (F · M) v (~F · ~M)
   *3. F   ACP
   *4. ~M   1,3 P
   *5. F v ~~M   3 Add
   *6. ~~F v ~~M   5 DN
   *7. ~(~F · ~M)   6 Dem

   *8. F · M   2,7 SC
   *9. M   8 Simp
  *10. M · ~M   9,4 Conj
  *11. ~F   10 Contr
   12. F ⊃ ~F   3-11 RCP
   13. ~F v ~F   12, DMI
   14. ~F   13, REP

4k

1. 1. R ⊃ (I v N)
    2. ~N
   *3. R   ACP
   *4. I v N   1,3 MP
   *5. I   2,4 SC
    6. R ⊃ I   3-5 RCP

3. 1. T ⊃ E
    2. E ⊃ ~B
    3. ~B ⊃ O
    4. T ⊃ ~B   1,2 HS
    5. T ⊃ O   3,4 HS

5. 1. C ⊃ [~B ⊃ (T v R)]
    2. R ⊃ (S v L)
    3. S ⊃ D
    4. L ⊃ B
    5. C
   *6.   ~D · ~B   ACP
   *7. ~B ⊃ (T v R)   1,5 MP
   *8. ~B   6 Simp
   *9. T v R   7,8 MP

  *10. ~L   4,8 MT
  *11. ~D   Simp
  *12. ~S   3,11 MT
  *13. ~S · ~L   10,12 Conj
  *14. ~(S v L)   13 DEM
  *15. ~R   2,14 MT
  *16. T   9,15 SC
   17. (~D · ~B) ⊃ T   9-16 RCP

45

CHAPTER FIVE

Begin by reading the opening section, "Writing Standard Form Statements", and "Diagrams" in Chapter
Five of the text. Then begin this chapter of the
study guide.

CATEGORICAL STATEMENTS

Many valid arguments employ no compound statements.

Every human is mortal	No philosopher is mortal
Socrates is a human	Some humans are philosophers
Socrates is mortal	Some humans are not mortal

No statement connectives ("and", "or", "if...then...", etc) are used. If we are
to analyze these, we must develop resources for representing the internal struc-
tures of statements that are not themselves composed of simpler statements.

     In sentences of the types in these arguments, we find proper names ("Socrates")
and common nouns or adjectives ("man", "mortal", "philosopher") linking the premises and conclusion. The common nouns and adjectives are used with "every",
"some" and "no" (the quantifier expressions) to construct noun phrases that serve
as the subjects of some of these statements. They also are used with "is" and
"is not" (or "is a" or "is not a" or "are" or "are not") to make the predicative
portion.

     Using "H" for "human" (or "humans") and "M" for "mortal" and "S" for "Socrates"
we can schematically present the six statement types that are most fundamental.
Each is associated with a diagram that indicates the class relationship expressed.
"O" represents an empty portion, "l" an occupied portion.

            A   Every H is M
                (All H are M.)

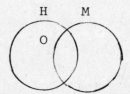

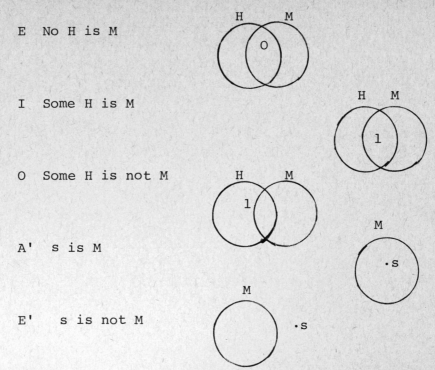

E   No H is M

I   Some H is M

O   Some H is not M

A'   s is M

E'   s is not M

    These are the standard forms for the six types of <u>categorical</u> <u>statement</u> central to traditional logic. In these examples, "H" is the <u>subject</u> <u>term</u> in the A, E, I and O statements, and "M" is the <u>predicate</u> <u>term</u> in all six.

    The A, E, I and O statements can be phrased in many ways in English. Some of the simpler ones are illustrated below. The statements are paraphrased into standard form. The subject term is marked by solid underlining, the predicate term by broken underlining.

A Statements.

All men are truck drivers. (Every <u>man</u> is a <u>truck</u> <u>driver</u>.)
Anyone with a truck can make money hauling dirt. (Every <u>person who has a truck</u>
    is an <u>individual who can make money hauling dirt</u>.)
Trucks need gas. (Every <u>truck</u> is a <u>thing that needs gas</u>.)
Those who drive trucks show no respect for those who don't.
    (Every <u>truck-driver</u> is an <u>individual who shows no respect for those who are</u>
    <u>not truck-drivers</u>)

E Statements.

Men are not born truck-drivers. (No <u>man</u> is an <u>individual who is born a truck-</u>
    <u>driver</u>.)
No one who drives a truck can marry my daughter. (No <u>person who drives a truck</u> is
    an <u>individual who can marry my daughter</u>.)
Trucks don't use coal. (No <u>truck</u> is a <u>thing that uses coal</u>.)

I Statements.

There are men who drive trucks (Some <u>man</u> is a <u>truck</u> <u>driver</u>.)
A truck-driver married my daughter. (Some <u>truck-driver</u> is a <u>man who married my</u>
    <u>daughter</u>.)

Trucks sometimes use diesel fuel. (Some <u>truck</u> is a <u>thing that uses diesel fuel</u>.)
A truck with a trailer passed. (Some <u>truck with a trailer</u> is a <u>thing that passed</u>.)

O Statements.

There are men who do not drive trucks. (Some <u>man</u> is not a <u>truck driver</u>.)
Some truck-drivers are not married. (Some <u>truck-driver</u> is not a <u>married individual</u>.
Truck-drivers have been known to obey the speed limit. (Some <u>truck-driver</u> is not
   a <u>speeder</u>.)
Some trucks don't need water. (Some <u>truck</u> is not a <u>thing that needs water</u>.)
Not every truck needs water. (Some <u>truck</u> is not a <u>thing that needs water</u>.)

<u>Exercise 5a</u>

For each of the following

    i.   If it is not in standard form, re-write it as an equivalent standard form
        statement.
   ii.   Identify the subject term and the predicate term.
  iii.   Indicate whether it is an A, E, I, O, A' or E' statement.
   iv.   Draw the corresponding Venn Diagram.

1.   All biologists are scientists.
2.   Any biologist is a scientist.
3.   Some scientists are not biologists.
4.   Not all scientists are biologists.
5.   The scientist studies nature.
6.   There are scientists who study nature.
7.   Only biologists study animals.
8.   Any biologist or chemist knows the nature of water.
9.   Some biologists know a great deal about carbon compounds.
10.   Some physicists know the most important things about all compounds.
11.   Some chemists with unusual specializations know a great deal about physics.
12.   No engineer is a scientist.
13.   No scientist can build a house.
14.   No scientist who does interesting research can build a house.
15.   There were not any biologists at the convention.
16.   Biologists don't study distant stars.
17.   Not every astronomer studies distant stars.
18.   None of the astronomers at the convention were physicists.
19.   John was at the convention.
20.   John is an astronomer.
21.   John is not a physicist.
22.   John will not attend another convention.
23. * John knows every physicist there.
24. * John knows some of the astronomers there.
25. * Some of the astronomers there know John.

Read the section of the text "Distribution", then
read the next section of the study guide.

DISTRIBUTION OF TERMS

When we assess arguments, it will be important to know which terms of a categorical statement are <u>distributed</u>. This can be represented in the following table.

Subject term distributed

	A: Every S is P. A': n is p	E: No S is P. E': n is not p.	
Predicate term Undistributed	I: Some S is P.	O: Some S is not P.	Predicate term Distributed

Subject term undistributed

Exercise 5b

For each of the sentences of 5a, indicate which terms are distributed.

Now read the section "Immediate Inference," then
read the next section of the study guide.

EQUIVALENCES

The following equivalences are characteristic of standard form sentences. ("$\overline{P}$" stands for "non-P".)

conversion
(E and I)

$$\frac{\text{No S is P}}{\text{No P is S}}$$

$$\frac{\text{Some S is P}}{\text{Some P is S}}$$

contraposition
(A and O)

$$\frac{\text{Every S is P}}{\text{Every } \overline{P} \text{ is } \overline{S}}$$

$$\frac{\text{Some S is not P}}{\text{Some } \overline{P} \text{ is not } \overline{S}}$$

obversion
(All six forms)

$$\frac{\text{Every S is P}}{\text{No S is } \overline{P}}$$

$$\frac{\text{No S is P}}{\text{Every S is } \overline{P}}$$

$$\frac{\text{Some S is P}}{\text{Some S is not } \overline{P}}$$

$$\frac{\text{Some S is not P}}{\text{Some S is } \overline{P}}$$

$$\frac{\text{n is P}}{\text{n is not } \overline{P}}$$

$$\frac{\text{n is not P}}{\text{n is } \overline{P}}$$

Exercise 5c

i. For each of the following, write two equivalent statements - the converse
    and the obverse.

    1. Some biologists are doctors.
    2. Some chemist is a doctor.
    3. No biologist is a butcher.
    4. No doctor is a chemist.
    5. Some doctor with a good practive wishes he were a biologist.
    6. Some biologist wishes he were a doctor with a good practice.
    7. No chemist will voluntarily associate with engineers.
    8. No physicist who knows a chemist will be at a loss for sources of infor-
        mation.

ii. For each of these, write two equivalent statements - the contrapositive and
     the obverse.

    1. All biologists study anatomy.
    2. Every doctor is an anatomy student.
    3. Some doctors do not study physics.
    4. Some biologist is not telling the truth.
    5. Any biologist with a good research proposal will be able to implement it.
    6. Any doctor with a good practice is envied.
    7. Some doctors do not have a good practice.
    8. Some doctors who do not have good practices are not able to support
        themselves.

iii. For each of the statements 1-18 of 5a, write two equivalent statements.

> Now read the section of the text "The Square of
> Opposition" and then read the next section of the
> study guide.

THE SQUARE OF OPPOSITION

The traditional square of opposition, presented in the text, presents in a
diagram several logical relationships. Some are equivalence relationships, others
are one-way interferences. These are presented individually below.

If we assume that S and P pick out non-empty classes, then the following
relations hold. (Those relying on this existence conditions are starred.)

Relations of contradiction:

A	Every S is P
not-O	It is not the case that some S is not P

O	Some S is not P
not-A	Not every S is P

E	No S is P
not-I	It is not the case that some S is P

I	Some S is P
not-E	It is not the case that no S is P

50

Subalternation (One-way implication relation)

*$\frac{A}{I}$	$\frac{\text{Every S is P}}{\text{Some S is P}}$	*$\frac{E}{O}$	$\frac{\text{No S is P}}{\text{Some S is non-p}}$

Contraries (Not both are true. One way implication relations.)

* $\frac{A}{\text{not-E}}$ $\frac{\text{Every S is P}}{\text{It is not the case that no S is P}}$

* $\frac{E}{\text{not-A}}$ $\frac{\text{No S is P}}{\text{Not every S is P}}$

Subcontraries (Not both are false. One-way implication relations.)

* $\frac{\text{not-E}}{O}$ $\frac{\text{It is not the case that some S is P}}{\text{Some S is not P}}$

* $\frac{\text{not-O}}{E}$ $\frac{\text{It is not the case that some S is not P}}{\text{Some S is P}}$

Exercise 5d

For each of the statements 1-18 of 5a, write a contradictory statement.

Exercise 5e

Which of the following pairs of statements are contradictory (i.e., one is true if and only if the other is false)? Which are contraries (i.e., not both can be true, but it is possible for both to be false)?

1. All women bear children.
   No women bear children.

2. Some women do not bear children.
   All women bear children.

3. Not every woman bears children.
   Every woman bears children.

4. Some women bear children.
   No woman bears children.

5. Only women bear children
   No child-bearers are women.

6. There are no women who bear children
   Some women bear children.

Now read the sections "Categorical Syllogisms", "Syllogistic Rules" and "Venn Diagrams for Syllogisms" in the text. Then read the next section of the study guide before doing Exercise 5C.

CATEGORICAL SYLLOGISMS

A syllogism has two standard form statements as premises, and a standard form statement as its conclusion. There are three terms. The <u>minor</u> term is the subject term of the conclusion, the <u>major</u> term is the predicate term of the conclusion, and the <u>middle</u> term appears in each premise but not in the conclusion.

> Every speeder is careless.
> <u>Some truck-drivers are speeders.</u>
> Some truck-drivers are careless.

"Speeder" is the <u>middle</u> term, "careless" (or "careless individual") is the <u>major</u> term, and "truck-driver" is the <u>minor</u> term.

The <u>Venn diagram</u> for a syllogism consists of three overlapping circles. Each circle represents the class of things picked out by one of the terms.

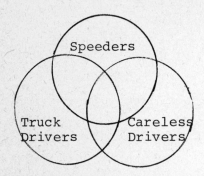

If we mark the circles as directed by the premises, we should find that they are marked appropriately for the conclusion when and only when the argument is valid. Thus

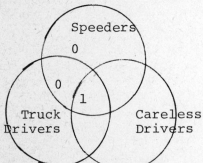

The first premise directs us to put in "0" twice to indicate that each of the areas within the speeders' circle, yet outside the circle for careless individuals, is empty. The second premise directs us to put a "1" in one of the areas within the overlap of the truck-drivers' circle and the speeders' circle. Since one of those areas is already marked with "0", we put the "1" in the other area. But that "1" tells us that the conclusion is true, i.e., that some truck-drivers are careless.

52

Exercise 5f

Using Venn diagrams (or some other techinique discussed in the text), determine whether these syllogisms are valid.

1. Some biologists have studied genetics, and some chemists are biologists, so some chemists have studied genetics.

2. Since all biologists are scientists, and some scientists are political activists, some biologists are political activists.

3. Some engineers are physicists. Thus, since all physicists are scientists, some engineers are scientists.

4. All physicists are scientists, and every scientist is devoted to the study of nature. Thus all physicists must be devoted to the study of nature.

5. No physicists are engineers, but some industrial researchers are physicists. So some industrial researchers are not engineers.

6. Any scientist who studies animals is a biologist. Ethologists study animals. So ethologists are biologists.

7. No scientist except a physicist needs to know calculus. No biologist needs to know calculus. So no biologist is a physicist.

8. Every physicist knows calculus. No biologists know calculus. Thus no biologist is a physicist.

9. No scientists doing interesting research were at the convention. Every scientist doing interesting research was working hard. Thus no one at the convention was working hard.

10. No biologist studies stars. Every astronomer studies stars. Thus biologists are not astronomers.

Now do Exercise 5C in the text. Then read the section
                    of the text entitled "Soriteses". Then read the next
                    section of the study guide.

SORITESES

    Not all arguments have just two premises. In cases of more complex arguments, syllogisms must be chained together. Such an argument is a Sorites. By pairing premises with a common term, we find syllogisms with conclusions that can be added to our stock of information and used to derive further conclusions. In a valid sorites we will eventually establish the main conclusion.

    P1 No one who drives carelessly is safe from the law.
    P2 Some truck-drivers speed.
    P3 Anyone who speeds is careless.
    C   Some truck-drivers are not safe from the law.

This conclusion can be established by these linked arguments.

    P3 Every speeder is a careless driver.
    P2 Some truck-driver is a speeder.
    C1 Some truck-driver is a careless driver
    P1 No careless driver is safe from the law.
    C   Some truck driver is not safe from the law.

53

For each set of premises, find a conclusion that validly follows. Use all of the premises in deriving the conclusion.

1. All biologists are scientists. No scientists are superstitious. No one who is not superstitious will visit a fortune-teller.

2. Some chemists are engineers. No engineers can join the Purity of Science association. All chemists are scientists.

3. Some chemists are engineers. All engineers are interested in business. Anyone interested in business will read the paper.

4. No physicists read the business section. All doctors read the business section. Some doctors are biologists.

5. Any physicist who has studied biology can solve our problem. Anyone who can solve our problem should be hired. Someone we interviewed is a physicist who has studied biology.

> Now read the section of the text entitled "Enthymemes",
> then read the next section of the study guide before
> doing the exercises at the end of the chapter in the
> text.

ENTHYMEMES

     In many cases, context or background information provides information that need not be explicitly stated.

> Since John is a truck-driver he must be
> opposed to raising fuel taxes.

It is clear that the speaker believes that all truck-drivers are opposed to raising gasoline taxes (if he intends his argument to be valid) . He need not explicitly state this missing premise. If he does not, his argument is an _enthymeme_ because it omits a premise.

     An argument is also enthymematic if it omits the conclusion.

> There is no need to ask John his opinion. He's a
> truck-driver and all truck-drivers are opposed to
> raising fuel taxes.

Exercise 5h

     Re-write each argument as a standard form syllogism or sorites, supply missing premises or conclusion if it is an enthymeme, then use Venn diagrams (or other technique) to determine if it is valid.

1. Since all biologists study anatomy, at least some scientists study anatomy.

2. John is a physicist and all physicists have studied calculus.

3. Anyone who has studied calculus can solve our problem, so John will be able to solve it.

4. Some doctors serve in developing nations, so at least some people serving in developing nations are well-educated.

5. All doctors are well-educated, so any doctor can tell you what Plato's theory of justice is.

6. Any well-educated person can tell you about Plato's Republic so there are people on my staff who will be able to tell you about it.

7. Biologists who are doctors never have time to study history. Everyone on this research staff is a biologist who is a doctor. So no one on this research staff will know how long Augustus Caesar was in power.

8. Any biologist who has studied the history of his field can tell you how Darwin devised his theory. Every biologist from our college has studied the history of his field. Thus all the biologists from our college know the story of Darwin's trip to the Galapagos.

5a.

1. Every <u>biologist</u> is a <u>scientist</u>. A.

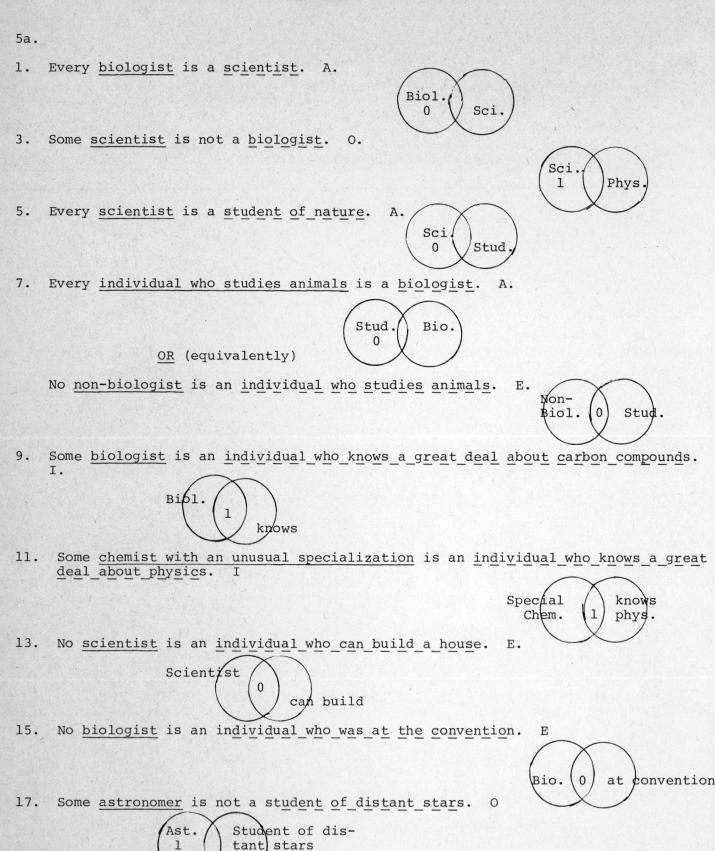

3. Some <u>scientist</u> is not a <u>biologist</u>. O.

5. Every <u>scientist</u> is a <u>student of nature</u>. A.

7. Every <u>individual who studies animals</u> is a <u>biologist</u>. A.

<u>OR</u> (equivalently)

No <u>non-biologist</u> is an <u>individual who studies animals</u>. E.

9. Some <u>biologist</u> is an <u>individual who knows a great deal</u> about <u>carbon compounds</u>.
I.

11. Some <u>chemist with an unusual specialization</u> is an <u>individual who knows a great deal about physics</u>. I

13. No <u>scientist</u> is an <u>individual who can build a house</u>. E.

15. No <u>biologist</u> is an <u>individual who was at the convention</u>. E

17. Some <u>astronomer</u> is not a <u>student of distant stars</u>. O

19. John is an individual_who_was_at_the convention. A'.

21. John is not a physicist. E'.

23. John is an individual_who_knows_every_physicist_there. A'.

OR

Every physicist there is an individual_who_is_known_by_John. A'.

25. Some astronomer there is an individual_who_knows_John. I.

OR

John is an_individual_who_is_known_by some_astronomers_there. A'.

5b

1. "Biologist".
3. "Biologist".
5. "Scientist".
7. "Individual who studies animals"(A)
            OR
    "Non-biologist" and "Individual who studies animals". (E)
9. None.
11. None.
13. "Scientist". "Individual who can build a house".
15. "Biologist". "Individual who was at the convention".
17. None.
19. "John".
21. "John". "Physicist".
23. "John". (A')
        OR
    "Physicist". (A)
25. None. (I)
        OR
    "John". (A')

57

i   1.   Some doctors are biologists.
Some biologist is not a non-doctor.

       3.   No butcher is a biologist.
Every butcher is a non-biologist.

       5.   Someone who wishes he were a biologist is a doctor with a good practice.
Some doctor with a good practice is not an individual who does not wish
he were a biologist.

       7.   No one who will voluntarily associate with engineers is a chemist.
Every chemist is an individual who will not voluntarily associate with
engineers.

ii   1.   Any who do not study anatomy are not biologists.
No biologist is not a student of anatomy.

       3.   Some who do not study physics are doctors.
Some doctor is not an individual who studies physics.

       5.   Anyone who cannot implement his research proposal is not a biologist with
a good research proposal.
No biologist with a good research proposal will be unable to implement it.

       7.   Some who do not have a good practice are not non-doctors.
Some doctor is an individual who does not have a good practice.

iii   1.   Every non-scientist is a non-biologist.
No biologist is a non-scientist.

       3.   Some non-biologist is a scientist.
Some scientist is a non-biologist.

       5.   Anyone who does not study nature is a non-scientist.
No scientist is not a student of nature.

       7.   Any non-biologist is an individual who does not study animals.
No individual who studies animals is a non-biologist.

       9.   There is someone who knows a great deal about carbon compounds who is a
biologist.
Some biologist is not an individual who knows little about carbon compounds

    11.   There is someone who knows a great deal about physics and who is a chemist
with an unusual specialization.
Some chemist with an unusual specialization is not an individual who knows
little about physics.

    13.   Every scientist is an individual who cannot build a house.
No scientist is not an individual who cannot build a house.

    15.   Every biologist is someone who was not at the convention.
No biologist is not someone who was not at the convention.

    17.   Someone who is not a student of distant stars is an astronomer.
Some astronomers are individuals who do not study distant stars.

5d

1. Some biologist is not a scientist.
3. Every scientist is a biologist.
5. Some scientists do not study nature.
7. Some individuals who study animals are not biologists.
9. No biologist knows a great deal about carbon compounds.
11. No chemist with an unusual specialization knows a great deal about physics.
13. Any scientist can build a house.
15. Some biologist was at the convention.
17. Every astronomer is a student of distant stars.

5e

1. Contrary
3. Contradictory
5. Contrary

5f

1.

Biologists

1?   1
  1?

Chemists   genetics students

Invalid.

3.

Physicists
0
1?
  1?
Engineers
        Scientists

Invalid.

5.

Physicists
      0
 1
   0
Industrial   Engineers
Researchers

Valid.

7.

Scientist who needs calculus
        0
   0
     0
Biologist   Physicists

Invalid.

9.

Doing interesting research
        0
  0
    0
 at the
convention   working hard

Invalid.

59

5g

1. No biologist will visit a fortune teller.
3. Some chemists read the paper.
5. Someone we interviewed should be hired.

5h

1. Every biologist is a student of anatomy.
   *Some scientist is a biologist
   Some scientist is a student of anatomy.

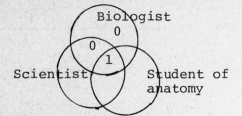

Valid

3. Every student of calculus is an individual who can solve our problem.
   *John is a student of calculus.
   John is an individual who can solve our problem.

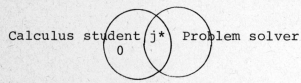

Valid

5. *Every well-educated individual is an individual who can tell you what Plato's Theory of justice is.
   Every doctor is a well-educated individual.
   Every doctor is an individual who can tell you what Plato's theory of justice is.

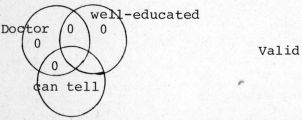

Valid

7. P1 No biologist who is a doctor is an individual who has had time to study history.
   P2 Every one on this research staff is a biologist who is a doctor.
       No one on this research staff has had time to study history.
       *No one who has not had time to study history will know how long Augustus Caesar was in power.
       No one on this research staff will know how long Augustus Caesar was in power.

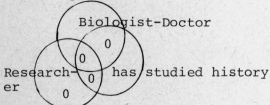

Valid

60

CHAPTER SIX

Begin by reading the opening section of Chapter Six.
Then read the following section of the study guide.

PREDICATE LOGIC: THE SIMPLE SYSTEM

In Chapter Six we study arguments in which the internal structure of non-compound statements is relevant to the evaluation of the argument. Thus we continue the study begun in Chapter Five. But here we will develop a system that is somewhat more flexible than traditional Aristotelian logic, that builds on what we learned about statement logic in Chapter Three, and that will prepare us for the study of the complete system of predicate logic - that is, of the core of modern logic - to be undertaken in Chapter Seven.

The simplest sort of statement is one that predicates some characteristic of some single, named individual.

            Al is a truck-driver
            Bill is friendly.
            Chicago is a city.

We will use capital letters to represent the predicative portions of such statements.

            T# ...is a truck-driver
            F# ...is friendly
            C# ...is a city

We will use lower-case letters (except "x", "y", "z", "u", "v" and "w") like proper names - to denote particular individuals.

            a# Al
            b# Bill
            c# Chicago

The sentences above will be represented symbolically by

            Ta
            Fb
            Cc

Some non-compound sentences are relational in character, saying something about two or more things.

> Detroit is east of Chicago.
> Al is taller than Ed.
> Frank hit Greg.

We will use capital letters to stand for these relations.

> Exy # x is east of y
> Txy # x is taller than y
> Hxy # x hit y

These sentences become

> Edc
> Tae
> Hfg.

In principle we could have three-place relations, as in "Detroit is between Buffalo and Chicago", and four-place relations as in "Detroit is farther from Buffalo than Chicago is from Milwaukee." But we will rarely need relations with more than two places.

Using the symbols of Chapters Three and Four, we can also construct truth-functional compounds of these sentences.

Massachusetts is not a city	~Cm
Chicago is not east of Buffalo	~Ecb
Buffalo is a city east of Chicago	Cb · Ebc
Buffalo and Detroit are east of Chicago.	Ebc · Edc

Exercise 6a

Symbolize the following simple sentences and truth-functional compounds of simple sentences.

1. John Wayne is an actor. (j# John Wayne, Ax#x is an actor.)
2. Mickey Rooney is not an actor. (m# Mickey Rooney)
3. John Wayne and Mickey Rooney are both actors.
4. Either John Wayne or Mickey Rooney will star in the picture. (Sx#x will star in the picture)
5. John Wayne will star in it and Mickey Rooney will miss it. (Mx#x will miss it)
6. John Wayne is taller than Mickey Rooney. (Txy#x is taller than y)
7. Mickey Rooney is not taller than John Wayne.
8. O. J. Simpson is taller than Mickey Rooney but not taller than John Wayne. (o# O. J. Simpson)
9. O. J. Simpson is an actor who is taller than John Wayne.
10. If John Wayne is taller than O. J. Simpson, then John Wayne will star in the movie and O. J. Simpson and Mickey Rooney will be sure to miss it.
11. John Wayne will star in the movie only if he is taller than O. J. Simpson and more famous than him too. (Mxy # x is more famous than y)
12. If O. J. Simpson is an actor who is famous, then if John Wayne does not star in the movie O. J. Simpson will. (Fx# x is famous)

> Now read the sections of the text "Placeholders and Quasi-names"
> and "Translating into Symbolic Form." Then read the next section
> of the study guide.

We now introduce a special sort of singular term - quasi-names. There are two types. A universal quasi-name is employed when we want to represent a claim that all objects have some characteristic. An existential quasi-name is used in representing a claim that at least one object or other has a certain characteristic (when it is not said which object has that characteristic).

Consider the following representation of a simple subject-predicate statement.

John Wayne is an actor.   Aj

The statement "Everything is an actor" says that every individual has the property that has just been attributed to John Wayne. We can represent that statement with a use of a universal quasi-name. This is formed by enclosing "x", "y", "z", "u", "v" or "w" in parentheses.

Everything is an actor.   A(x)

Of course, we are unlikely to want to make such a general claim.

A much more typical statement of a universal sort would be something like "Every actor has a good memory." This still tells us something about every individual; if that individual is an actor, then she or he has a good memory. Thus, using " ⊃ "or " v " we get:

Every actor has a good memory.
$A(x) \supset M(x)$
$\sim A(x) \vee M(x)$

If John Wayne is an actor, he has a good memory.
$Aj \supset Mj$
$\sim Aj \vee Mj$

"(x)" is to be interpreted as a term that might name any object whatsoever. It is claimed that no matter what it might refer to, the statement would be true. Thus if the universal claim "Every actor has a good memory" is true, then all of these should be true:

If Mickey Rooney is an actor, then he has a good memory.
$Am \supset Mm$
$\sim Am \vee Mm$

If Jimmy Carter is an actor, then he has a good memory.
$Ac \supset Mc$
$\sim Ac \vee Mc$

If Detroit is an actor, then Detroit has a good memory.
$Ad \supset Md$
$\sim Ad \vee Md$

All of these will be true if the original universal statement is true. Either an individual is not an actor, or else the individual has a good memory. Thus we use the universal quasi-name and the " ⊃ " (or "~" and "v") in representing most claims involving words like "every", "all", "any", "each".

If we want to say "Someone is an actor" we must use an existential quasi-name. This is formed like a universal quasi-name, but with square brackets.

Someone is an actor.   A[x]

This says that at least one individual is an actor. Again, a more typical claim will involve more than one predicate. Thus

Some actor is rich. $A[x] \cdot R[x]$

63

This says that at least one individual is both an actor and rich. There is something that "x" might name such that the conjunction would be true. At least one
of these is true (if we make a complete list.)

```
          Aj · Rj
          Ac · Rc
          Am · Rm
          Ad · Rd
            etc.
               .
               .
               .
```

If the original sentence -"A[x] · R[x]"- is true, then there must be at least
one individual to which the predicates "A" and "R" apply.

   "There are rich actors", "Some actor is rich", "Some actors are rich", and
"At least one actor is rich" are among the most common statements that will be
represented by "A[x] · R[x]".

   The A, E, I and O forms of Aristotelian logic will be represented in the
following way.

A:	Every actor is rich.	A(x) ⊃ R(x)	or	~A(x) v R(x)
E:	No actor is rich.	A(x) ⊃ ~R(x)	or	~A(x) v ~R(x)
I:	Some actor is rich.	A[x] · R[x]		
O:	Some actor is not rich.	A[x] · ~R[x]		

   The negation of a sentence with a quasi-name cannot be made simply by putting
"~" before the sentence. We must switch quasi-names (and perhaps more) as well.

There is someone who is an actor.	A[x]
There is not someone who is an actor. (No one is an actor) (Everyone is a non-actor)	~A(x)
Everyone is an actor	A(x)
Not everyone is an actor (Someone is a non-actor)	~A[x]

Exercise 6b

i. Symbolize these sentences.

   1. All truck-drivers speed. (Tx #x is a truck-driver, Sx #x speeds)

   2. Some truck-drivers don't speed.

   3. Not all truck-drivers speed.

   4. No truck-drivers speed.

   5. Some truck-drivers speed and drive carelessly. (Cx # x drives carelessly)

   6. Some truck-drivers who speed are careless.

   7. No truck-driver who speeds is careless.

   8. Any truck-driver who speeds is a careless driver.

64

9.   Someone knows Al.   (Kxy # x knows y)

10.   Al knows everyone.

11.   Everyone who Al knows speeds.

12.   Some truck-drivers know Al.

13.   Al knows himself.

14.   Everyone knows himself.

15.   There is someone who knows himself.

> Read the section "Rules for Changing Terms" in the
> text, and then read the next section of the study
> guide.

SIMPLE INFERENCES

   Given the interpretation of our quasi-names, certain inferences involving them
are obviously valid and can form the beginnings of a deductive system.

UN

$$\frac{A(x)}{An}$$ Whatever is true of everything must be true of each named individual.

This allows us to take any sentence with a universal quasi-name and replace all
occurences of that name by some single proper name.

NP

$$\frac{An}{A[x]}$$ Whatever is true of a particular named object is true of something.

This allows us to replace each occurence of some proper name by an existential
quasi-name. We must use an existential quasi-name that has not been used previously
in the proof. (The reason is given in the text.)

UP

$$\frac{A(x)}{A[x]}$$ Whatever is true of everything is true of something.

This simply combines UN and NP (allowing the inference even when we do not know the
names of the relevant objects) . It is worth noting that UP is valid only if there
exists at least one object.

When added to the rules for statement logic, these three rules provide the resources for doing many derivations. In subsequent sections we will show how the inferences of traditional Aristotelian logic can be done very simply with the rules just given. (In fact, NP is not even needed for that.)

We can familiarize ourselves with the rules by examining a few simple derivations.

1. 1. Ea · Da   E[x] · ~C[x]?
    2. ~Da v ~Ca
    3. Ea · ~Ca   1,2 CJ
    4. E[x] · ~C[x]   3 NP

2. 1. ~B(x) v C(x)
    2. ~A(x) v B(x)   Aa?
    3. ~Ca
    4. ~Ba v Ca   1 UN
    5. ~Ba   3,4 SC
    6. ~Aa v Ba   2 UN
    7. ~Aa   5,6 SC

3. 1. ~A(x) v B(x)   C[x] · B[x]?
    2. A[x] · C[x]
    3. ~A[x] v B[x]   1 UP
    4. C[x] · B[x]   2,3 CJ

Exercise 6c

Do a derivation to establish the proposed conclusion.

1. ~A(x) v B(x)
    ~B(x) v C(x)   ~A(x) v C(x)?

2. ~Ea
    ~A(x) v ~B(x) v C(x)   ~Aa v Da v ~Ba?
    ~C(x) v D(x) v E(x)

3. Aa · Ba
    ~A(x) v C(x)   B[x] · D[x]?
    ~C(x) v D(x)

4. ~A(x) v C(x)
    ~A(x) v B(x)   ~A(x) v D(x)?
    ~C(x) v ~B(x) v D(x)

5. ~Aa v ~B(x) v D(x)
    ~B(x) v ~D(x) v C(x)   ~Aa v ~B(x) v C(x)?

6. ~Aa v ~B(x) v D(x)
    ~B(x) v A(x)   ~B(x) v D(x)?
    Ba

7. Ba · Bb
    ~Da v Gb   B[x] · D[x] · G[x]?
    ~B(x) v D(x)

8. Rab
    ~R(x)b v F(x)   F[x] · ~F[y]?
    ~Fb

9. F[x] · ~G[x]
    ~H(x) v G(x)   F[x] · K[x]?
    H(x) v K(x)

66

10. F[x] · G[x]
    F[y] · ~G[y]
    ~G(x) v H(x)   (F[x] · H[x]) · (F[y] · ~H[y])?
    ~H(x) v G(x)

11. ~F(x) v Ra(x)
    Fb · Ha   H[y] · R[y][x]?

12. F[x] · G[y] · R[x][y]
    ~F(x) v H(x)   H[x] · K[y] · R[x][y]?
    ~G(x) v K(x)

13. F[x] · G[x]
    ~Ha v ~F(x) v G(x)   ~F(x) v G(x)?
    Ha v ~G(x)

14. Fa · Ga
    G[x] · ~H[x]   (F[y] · G[y]) · (~F[x] · G[x])?
    ~F(x) v H(x)

15. A[x] · B[x]
    ~A(x) v Ba   Ba . Ca?
    ~B(x) v C(x)

> Read "Syllogistic Logic" and "Equivalent Statements"
> in the text. Then read the next section of the
> study guide.

EQUIVALENCES

The familiar equivalence rules of statement logic are sufficient to establish
the elementary equivalences of Aristotelian logic.

Conversion

To warrent the conversion inferences, we need only the commutativity rule.

No S is P	$\sim$S(x) v $\sim$P(x)
No P is S	$\sim$P(x) v $\sim$S(x)

Some S is P	S[x] · P[x]
Some P is S	P[x] · S[x]

Contraposition

Only commutativity and double negation are required.

Every S is P	$\sim$S(x) v P(x)
Every $\overline{P}$ is $\overline{S}$	$\sim\sim$P(x) v $\sim$S(x)

Some S is not P	S[x] · $\sim$P[x]
Some $\overline{P}$ is not $\overline{S}$	$\sim$P[x] · $\sim\sim$S[x]

Obversion

Every S is P	$\sim$S(x) v P(x)
No S is $\overline{P}$	$\sim$S(x) v $\sim\sim$P(x)
No S is P	$\sim$S(x) v $\sim$P(x)
Every S is $\overline{P}$	$\sim$S(x) v $\sim$P(x)
Some S is P	S[x] · P[x]
Some S is not $\overline{P}$	S[x] · $\sim\sim$P[x]
Some S is not P	S[x] · $\sim$P[x]
Some S is $\overline{P}$	S[x] · $\sim$P[x]
n is P	Pn
n is not $\overline{P}$	$\sim\sim$Pn
n is not P	$\sim$Pn
n is $\overline{P}$	$\sim$Pn

In each case of obversion, either the equivalent Aristotelian sentences are represented in the same way, or else double negation is sufficient to guarantee the equivalence.

Exercise 6d

Use our system based on quasi-names to symbolize the sentences of Exercise 5c. For the sentences of part i, symbolize the obverse and converse, and demonstrate their equivalence. For those of part ii, symbolize the obverse and contrapositive and show their equivalence.

SYLLOGISMS

Using UN, UP and the rules of the simple system of statement logic (Chapter Three) we can derive the conclusion from the premises in any valid syllogism. This is presented case by case in the text.

Exercise 6e

Symbolize the argument and derive the conclusion in each of the syllogisms of Exercise 5f.

SORITESES

A sorites can now be treated straightforwardly as an argument with more than two premises. We simply use our system of deductive rules to derive (or refute) the conclusion.

Symbolize the soriteses of Exercise 5g and derive the appropriate conclusion in each case. Symbolize the enthymemes of 5h (including the suppressed premise) and derive the conclusion.

NON-SYLLOGISTIC ARGUMENTS

An argument may be non-syllogistic in any of three ways. It might involve sentential compounds of standard form sentences (like "If some famous actors have a party, then all of the fan magazine readers find out") , it might contain relational statements (like "Buffalo is east of Chicago" or "Honolulu is west of everything") or it might contain sentences with more than one quantifier (like "Everybody loves somebody" or "There is a city that is west of everything") .

The full system of predicate logic to be developed in the next chapter is adequate to deal with all of these types of argument. But even the simple system developed here can deal with the first two types of argument and with some arguments of the third type.

Here are some relatively simple arguments that we can deal with easily, but which are beyond the scope of Aristotelian syllogism.

1. Carter defeated Ford. So Carter defeated someone and there is someone who defeated Ford.

1.	Dcf	
2.	Dc[x]	1NP
3.	D[y]f	1 NP
4.	Dc[x] · D[y]f	2,3 Conj.

2. Every person who knows anyone he can blackmail is in a position to earn lots of money. Adams knows Baker and can blackmail him. So Adams is in a position to earn a lot of money.

   Kxy # x knows y
   Bxy # x can blackmail y
   Ex # x is in a position to earn

1.	(K(x)(y) · B(x)(y)) ⊃ E(x)	Ea
2.	Kab · Bab	
3.	(Ka(y) · Ba(y)) ⊃ Ea	1 UN
4.	(Kab · Bab) ⊃ Ea	3 UN
5.	Ea	2,4 MP

3. If anyone Baker knows has read that story, that person can blackmail Baker. Baker knows Adams, and Adams has read that story. So Adams can blackmail someone.

   Kxy # x knows y
   Bxy # x can blackmail y
   Rx # x has read that story

1.	(Kb(x) · R(x)) ⊃ B(x)b		5.	Kba · Ra	2,3 Conj.
2.	Kba		6.	Bab	4,5 MP
3.	Ra		7.	Ba[x]	6 NP
4.	(Kba · Ra) ⊃ Bab	1UN			

In the exercises for this chapter, there is one rule of technical convenience that may be required for some arguments. This is:

UU $\dfrac{A(x)}{A(y)}$ We may switch letters in a universal quasi-name, so long as it is done throughout the statement

1. A(x) ⊃ B(x)   A(x) ?
2. ~B(y)
3. ~B(x)   2 UU
4. ~A(x)   1,3 MT

Exercise 6g

Symbolize and derive the conclusion. At least some are enthymemes and missing premises or conclusion must be supplied.

1. Scientists study nature. Anyone who studies nature is deserving of praise. Thus all biologists and chemists are deserving of praise.

2. If Bill gets a grant, all of the biologists will be pleased. So if Bill gets a grant, Al will be pleased.

3. All of Bill's children are biologists. Carol is Bill's daughter. So Carol must be a biologist.

4. Everyone in the society is a biologist or a chemist. No biologists are here. So everyone here must be a chemist.

5. Of Bill's children, only his daughters are biologists. Al is Bill's son. So Al is not a biologist.

6. Any one of Bill's daughters who wins a Nobel Prize will please Bill. Alice is one of BIll's children and she will win the Nobel Prize if she is fairly recognized. Thus if Alice is fairly recognized, she will please Bill.

REFUTATION

Statement	Refuted by
Every A is B	n is A but not B
A(x) ⊃ B(x)	An · ~Bn
~A(x) v B(x)	
	or
	Some A is not B
	A[x] · ~B[x]
No A is B	n is A and B
A(x) ⊃ ~B(x)	An · Bn
~A(x) v ~B(x)	
	or
	Some A is B
	A[x] · B[x]

```
Some A is B                              No A is B
A[x] · B[x]                                A(x) ⊃ ~B(x)
                                           ~A(x) v ~B(x)

                                                 or

                                         No B is A
                                           B(x) ⊃ ~A(x)
                                           ~B(x) v ~A(x)

                                                 or

                                         Nothing is A
                                           ~A(x)

                                                 or

                                         Nothing is B
                                           ~B(x)

Some A is not B                          Every A is B
A[x] · ~B[x]                               A(x) ⊃ B(x)
                                           ~A(x) v B(x)

                                                 or

                                         Every non-B is non-A
                                           ~B(x) ⊃ ~A(x)
                                           B(x) v ~A(x)

                                                 or

                                         Nothing is A
                                           ~A(x)

                                                 or

                                         Everything is B
                                           B(x)
```

In general, the statements that refute "A[x] · B[x]" or "A[x] · ~B[x]" are much more difficult to prove than those that refute the general statements "A(x) ⊃ B(x)" or "A(x) ⊃ ~B(x)".

Exercise 6i

Establish or refute the proposed conclusion in each.

Symbols

```
1.  ~A(x) v B(x)
    ~B(x) v C(x)              A[x] · ~C[x]?

2.  A[x] · C[x]
    ~D(x) v ~C(x)            ~A(x) v D(x)?

3.  ~R(x)(y) v F(x)
    ~G(x) v ~F(x)            Raa?
      Ga
```

71

4. ~F(x) v ~G(x)   F[x] · R[x][y]?
    ~R(x)(y) v G(x)

5. ~A(x) v B(x)   A[x] · C[y] · R[x][y]?
    ~B(x) v ~C(y) v R(x)(y)
    Aa · Cb

6. ~F(x) v ~G(y) v R(x)(y)   Raa?
    Fa · Ga

AN IMPORTANT RELATION BETWEEN PROOFS AND REFUTATIONS

In any valid proof, if the premises are true, the conclusion must be true.
Thus if the conclusion is not true, at least one premise is not true. Whenever
we have a valid proof of a conclusion C from some premises, we can construct a
valid refutation of one of the premises by making the negation of C (not-C) a premise along with the others.

If

$$P_1$$
$$\frac{P_2}{C}$$

is a valid proof, then

$$P_1$$

not-C

can serve as a premises in a valid refutation of P_2. Similarly

$$P_2$$

not-C

can serve as a premises in a valid refutation of P_1. (Of course, only one of these
can be sound, and determining which is sound is usually the interesting part.)

Science is wrong or else we have no free will.
Science is not wrong
We have no free will

Science is wrong or else we have no free will
We have free will
Science is wrong

Science is not wrong
We have free will
It is not true either that science is wrong or that we have no
free will.

Each of these is a valid proof, and each validly refutes a premise that occurs
in the other two. At most one is sound.

ANSWERS

6a

1. Aj
3. Aj · Am
5. Sj · Mm

7. ~Tmj
9. Ao · Toj
11. Sj ⊃ (Tjo · Mjo)

6b

1. T(x) ⊃ S(x)   or   ~T(x) v S(x)
3. T[x] · ~S[x]
5. T[x] · S[x] · C[x]
7. (T (x) · S(x)) ⊃ ~C(x)   or   ~T(x) v ~S(x) v ~C(x)
9. K[x]a
11. Ka(x) ⊃ S(x)   or   ~Ka(x) v S(x)
13. Kaa
15. K[x][x]

6c

1. 1. ~A(x) v B(x)
    2. ~B(x) v C(x)
    3. ~A(x) v C(x)   1,2 CC

3. 1. Aa · Bb
    2. ~A(x) v C(x)
    3. ~C(x) v D(x)
    4. ~Aa v Ca   2UN

5. ~Ca v Da   3 UN
6. ~Aa v Da   4,5 CC
7. Ba · Da   1,4 CJ

5. 1. ~Aa v ~B(x) v D(x)
    2. ~B(x) v A(x)
    3. Ba

4. ~Ba v Aa   2 UN
5. Aa   3,4 SC
6. ~B(x) v D(x)   1,5 SC

7. 1. Ba · Bb
    2. ~Da v Gb
    3. ~B(x) v D(x)
    4. ~Ba v Da   3 UN
    5. Bb · Da   1,4 CJ
    6. Bb · Gb   2,5 CJ

7. ~Bb v Db
8. Bb
9. Db
10. Bb · Gb · Db
11. Bb · Db · Gb
12. B[x] · D[x] · G[x]

3 UN
6 Simp
7,8 SC
6,9 Conj
10 Comm
11 NP

9. 1. F[x] · ~G[x]
    2. ~H(x) v G(x)
    3. H(x) v K(x)
    4. ~H[x] v G[x]   2 UP

5. F[x] · ~H[x]   1,4 CJ
6. H[x] v K[x]   3 UP
7. F[x] · K[x]   5,6 CJ

11. 1. ~F(x) v Ra(x)
    2. Fb · Ha
    3. ~Fb v Rab   1 UN

4. Ha · Rab   2,3 CJ
5. H[y] · R[y]b   4 NP
6. H[y] · R[y][x]   5 NP

13. 1. F[x] · G[x]
    2. ~Ha v ~F(x) v G(x)
    3. Ha v ~G(x)
    4. Ha v ~G[x]   3 UP

5. F[x] · Ha   1, 4 CJ
6. Ha   5 Simp
7. ~F(x) v G(x)   2,6 SC

15. 1. A[x] · B[x]
    2. ~A(x) v Ba
    3. ~B(x) v C(x)
    4. ~A[x] v Ba   2 UP
    5. A[x]   1 Simp

6. Ba   4,5 SC
7. ~Ba v Ca   3 UN
8. Ca   6,7 SC
9. Ba · Ca   8 Conj

6g

1.   1.   ~S(x) v N(x)   5.   ~C(x) v N(x)   1,4 CC
      2.   ~N(x) v D(x)   6.   ~C(x) v D(x)   2,5 CC
     *3.   ~B(x) v S(x)   7.   ~B(x) v N(x)   1,3 CC
     *4.   ~C(x) v S(x)   8.   ~B(x) v D(x)   2,7 CC

3.   1.   ~C(x)b v B(x)   5.   Ccb   2,4 SC
      2.   Dcb   6.   ~Ccb v Bc   1 UN
     *3.   ~D(x)b v C(x)b   7.   Bc
      4.   ~Dcb v Ccb   3 UN

5.   1.   ~C(x)b v ~B(x) v D(x)b
      2.   Sab
     *3.   ~S(x)b v ~D(x)b
     *4.   ~S(x)b v C(x)b
      5.   ~Sab v ~Dab   3 UN
      6.   ~Cab v ~Ba v Dab   1 UN
      7.   ~Cab v ~Ba v ~Sab   5,6 CC
      8.   ~Cab v ~Ba   2,7 SC
      9.   ~Sab v Cab   4 UN
     10.   Cab   2,9 SC
     11.   ~Ba   8,10 SC

6i

1.   1.   ~A(x) v B(x)
      2.   ~B(x) v C(x)
      3.   ~A(x) v C(x)   1,2 CC
            Refutes "A[x] · ~C[x]."

3.   1.   ~R(x)(y) v F(x)   5.   ~Ga v ~Ra(y)   4 UN
      2.   ~G(x) v ~F(x)   6.   ~Ga v ~Raa   5 UN
      3.   Ga   7.   ~Raa   3,6 SC
      4.   ~G(x) v ~R(x)(y) 1,2 CC   Refutes "Raa".

5.   1.   ~A(x) v B(x)
      2.   ~B(x) v ~C(y) v R(x)(y)
      3.   Aa · Cb
      4.   ~Aa v Ba   1 UN
      5.   ~Ba v ~C(y) v Ra(y)   2 UN
      6.   Aa   3 Simp
      7.   Ba   4,6 SC
      8.   ~C(y) v Ra(y)   5,7 SC
      9.   Cb   3 Simp
     10.   ~Cb v Rab   8 UN
     11.   Rab   9,10 SC
     12.   Aa · Cb · Rab   3,11 Conj
     13.   A[x] · Cb · R[x]b   12 NP
     14.   A[x] · C[y] · R[x][y]   13 NP

CHAPTER SEVEN

First read the opening section and the
section entitled "Quantifiers" in the
text. Then read the following section
of the study guide.

QUANTIFIERS

    We now introduce something new for representing statements involving "every",
"some", and related words. These are the <u>universal</u> and <u>existential</u> <u>quantifiers</u>.

    In simple sentences, quantifiers and quasi-names look like nothing more than
variants upon one another. As we did in Chapter Six, we can use universal quasi-
names in our representation of general statements (statements that tell us something about each individual object). In a simple universal statement like "Everything is material" this is simply

$$M(x).$$

The universal quasi-name indicates that no matter what individual might be named
by the universal term, the statement would be true. A more typical general statement like "All actors are rich" also tells us something about each individual
object x - that if x is an actor, then x is rich.   The conditional

$$A(x) \supset R(x)$$

would be true no matter what the universal term might refer to.

    A <u>universal</u> <u>quantifier</u> will be formed as follows - an upside-down capital "A"
followed by an "x", "y", "z", "u", "v" or "w", within parentheses

$$(\forall x)$$
$$(\forall y)$$
etc.

This is put at the beginning of a sentence and makes a claim of universal applica-
tion for what follows.

$$(\forall x)(x \text{ is material})$$
"Consider any object at all; it is material.

75

"All actors are rich" will be

$$(\forall x)(Ax \supset Rx)$$

"Consider any object at all; if it is an actor, then it is rich."

What follows the quantifier must be true of every object if the sentence is to be true.

Particular statements like "Some actors are rich" have been represented with existential quasi-names.

$$A[x] \cdot R[x]$$

The _existential_ _quantifier_ will now be used. It is formed like the universal quantifier, but with "$\exists$" rather than "$\forall$". It says that there is some individual or other of which the rest of the sentence is true.

$$(\exists x)(Ax \cdot Rx)$$

> "There is some individual of the following
> sort; it is an actor and it is rich"

For the sentence to be true, what follows the quantifier must be true of at least one individual.

So far there is no apparent advantage to the quantifiers over quasi-names. But by placing the quantifiers at the beginning of a sentence, we open up the possibility of ordering them, and thus using order as a relevant feature in our interpretation of a statement. Consider these sentences

> Everything has an antidote.
> There is an antidote for everything.

Although each of the English sentences may be ambigous, there are clearly two different claims that might be made. One is that each thing has its antidote - but perhaps different antidotes for different things. The other is that there is a single, universal antidote. Quasi-names, unfortunately, permit no differentiatio here. Suppose

Axy # x is an antidote for y.

Employing quasi-names, we would get

A [x](y)

no matter which of these claims we try to represent.

Quantifiers permit us to make a distinction here, between

> $$(\forall y)(\exists x)(Axy)$$
>
> "Pick any object y; there is some object x
> that is an antidote for y" i.e. "Each thing
> has its antidote"
>
> $$(\exists x)(\forall y)(Axy)$$
>
> "There is something x of which the following is
> true; x is an antidote for everything"

By varying the order of the quantifiers, we get statements that differ in meaning in the appropriate way.

With the addition of quantifiers, we achieve another desirable goal. Writing "~" before a statement p produces a statement that is the contradictory of p. This does not hold for statements with quasi-names. "~F(x)" ("Everything is non-F") is not the contradictory of "F(x)" ("Everything is F"). They are contraries. The contradictory of "F(x)" is "~F[x]" ("Something is not F").

The addition of the quantifiers allows us to resolve this. "~(∀x)(Fx)" ("Not everything is F") is the contradictory of "(∀x)(Fx)" ("Everything is F"). The contrary that was represented by "~F(x)" when we employed quasi-names is now to be represented by "(∀x)(~Fx)" ("Everything is non-F" or "Nothing is F"). The relative order of the quantifier and "~" makes a difference.

Variables As Pronouns

The singular terms "x", "y", etc. are called "variables". They occur first within the quantifier and then later as pronouns referring back to the quantifier. "Consider any individual; if it is an actor, it is rich." That sentence uses English pronouns in the way we will use these variables - "Consider any individual x; if x is an actor, x is rich." Our large supply of such pronouns makes cross-reference clear even in complex cases.

> "For every number there is one greater"
> $(x)(\exists y)(Gyx)$

> "If one number is greater than a second, and the second is greater than a third, then the first is greater than the third."
> $(x)(y)(z)\ [(Gxy \cdot Gyz) \supset Gxz]$

Exercise 7a

i. Using the universal and existential quantifiers, symbolize the sentences of Exercise 6b. (For additional practice, symbolize the sentences of Exercise 5a, 5c and 5e.)

ii. Symbolize the following sentences.

1. Any engineer is a mathematician. (Ex, Mx)
2. All engineers are mathematicians.
3. Each engineer is a mathematician.
4. Whoever is an engineer is a mathematician.
5. Engineers are mathematicians.
6. No one but a mathematician is an engineer.
7. Only engineers are mathematicians.
8. Some philosophers are mathematicians. (Fx # x is a philosopher)
9. There are philosophers who are not mathematicians.
10. There are philosophers and there are mathematicians.
11. Some philosophers are mathematicians and some are physicists.
    (Px # x is a physicist)
12. No philosopher is both a physicist and a moral theorist.
    (Mx # x is a moral theorist)
13. Einstein was a physicist and musicologist.
    (Sx # x is (or was) a musicologist)
14. Bohr was not an American physicist.
    (Ax # x is an American)
15. Physicists and philosophers are deep thinkers.
    (Dx # x is a deep thinker)

16. Not all deep thinkers are physicists or philosophers.
17. There are philosophers who are also physicists and mathematicians.
18. Some physicists know more than Bohr.
    (Kxy # x knows more than y)
19. Bohr knows more than any philosopher.
20. There's a philosopher who knows more than Bohr and more than Einstein.
21. Anyone knows more than someone.
22. Anyone who knows more than Bohr and more than Einstein should be famous.
    (Bx # x should be famous)
23. Every physicist knows more than some philosophers.
24. Some physicists know more than any philosopher.
25. There is an American philosopher who knows more than any physicist
    and more than any mathematician.
26. There is a mathematician who knows more than any American mathematician
    and more than some physicists.

Next read the sections of the text entitled
"Quantifiers and Quasi-names," "Instantiation
and Generalization Rules," and "Restrictions
on the Instantiation and Generalization Rules."
Then read the next three sections of this
study guide.

INSTANTIATION AND GENERALIZATION RULES

The deductive system for predicate logic builds upon the system for statement logic developed in Chapters Three and Four and also upon the system involving quasi-names developed in Chapter Six. Our principal new rules simply allow the dropping or introducing of quantifiers. Most other inferences are those familiar from statement logic.

Let us begin with the least problematic of these rules.

Universal	$(\forall w)(Zw)$
Instantiation	$Z(w)$

We can drop a universal quantifier and use the corresponding universal quasi-name to replace each of the "pronouns" that referred back to that quantifier. For example

    1. $(\forall x)(Ax \supset Rx)$
    2. $A(x) \supset R(x)$ 1UI

Note that by employing the rule UN with UI, we can go on to infer each instance of the quantified statement.

    1. $(\forall x)(Ax \supset Rx)$
    2. $A(x) \supset R(x)$ 1UI
    3. $Aj \supset Rj$ 2UN
    4. $Ac \supset Rc$ 2UN   etc.

If all actors are rich, then if John Wayne is an actor, he is rich, and if Jimmy Carter is an actor, then he is rich. The use of UI and UN allows us to apply these universal claims to any named individual.

Another unproblematic rule is _existential generalization_.

Existential	$Z[w]$
Generalization	$(\exists w)(Zw)$

If we know that a particular individual has a certain characteristic, we must be permitted to infer that there is something that has that characteristic. We use NP and EG to do this. Thus if we know that John Wayne is a rich actor

$$1. \quad Aj \cdot Rj$$

we can prove that there are some rich actors.

$$
\begin{array}{lll}
2. & A[x] \cdot R[x] & 1NP \\
3. & (\exists x)(Ax \cdot Rx) & 2\ EG.
\end{array}
$$

Retaining our quasi-names and the rules involving them will enable us to develop a relatively uncomplicated system of predicate logic when we add additional rules.

Exercise 7b

Using UI, EG, NP, and UN, together with the rules of statement logic, prove that each is valid.

1. $(\forall x)(Ax \supset Bx)$
    $(\forall x)(Bx \supset Cx)$
    $\underline{\sim Ca}$
    $\quad \sim Aa$

2. $Da \cdot Ea$
    $Ea \supset (Ga \lor Fa)$
    $Fa \supset Ca$
    $\underline{Da \supset \sim Ca}$
    $(\exists x)(Gx \cdot Ex)$

3. $Fb \cdot Gb$
    $(\forall x)(Gx \supset Rx)$
    $\underline{(\forall x)[(Rx \cdot Fx) \supset Mx]}$
    $(\exists x)(Mx)$

4. $(\forall x)[(Fx \cdot Gx) \supset Hx]$
    $(\forall x)[Hx \supset (Dx \lor Ex)]$
    $\underline{\sim Ea}$
    $(Fa \cdot \sim Da) \supset \sim Ga$

5. $Fa \cdot Fb$
    $(\forall x)(Fx \supset Dx)$
    $\underline{(Da \cdot Ea) \supset Gb}$
    $Ea \supset (\exists x)(Dx \cdot Gx)$

6. Rab
    $\underline{(\exists x)(Rxb) \supset (\forall x)(Rxb)}$
    Rbb

7. Rab
    $(\forall x)(Rxb \supset Fx)$
    $\underline{\sim Fb}$
    $(\exists x)(Fx) \cdot (\exists y)(\sim Fy)$

8. $(\forall x)(Ax \supset Bx)$
    $\underline{Ad \cdot Cd}$
    $(\forall x)(Cx \supset Dx) \supset (\exists y)(By \cdot Dy)$

9. $(\forall x)(Fx \supset Gx)$
    $(\forall x)(\forall y)[(\sim Fx \cdot Gy) \supset Rxy]$
    $(\forall x)(Hx \supset \sim Gx)$
    $\underline{Ha \cdot Fb}$
    $(\exists x)(\sim Hx \cdot Rax)$

10. $\underline{(\forall x)(Rxb)}$
    $(\exists y)(Ray)$

Proceed to the next section of the study guide.

EXISTENTIAL INSTANTIATION

EI, like UI, allows for the dropping of a quantifier, marking each of the pronoun places with an <u>existential</u> <u>quasi-name</u> to indicate which quantifier is dropped.

$$
\begin{array}{ll}
\text{Existential} & \dfrac{(\exists w)(Zw)}{Z[w]} \\
\text{Instantiation} &
\end{array}
$$

The existential quasi-name tells us, as the existential quantifier does, that "Z" is true of some individual or other.

In proofs the existential quasi-name is used as though it named one of the individuals of which "Z" is true. Using the same name for different individuals would be confusing, and so we must not allow the use of the same existential quasi-name in two separate EI steps. If this restriction were violated from "(∃x)(Cx)" ("There are cats") and "(∃x)(~Cx)" ("There are things that are non-cats") one could infer (∃x)(Cx · ~Cx)" ("There are cats that are not cats.")

This would occur in the following way:

1.	(∃x)(Cx)		
2.	(∃x)(~Cx)		
3.	C[x]	1 EI	
4.	~C[x]	2 EI	NOT PERMITTED
5.	C[x] · ~C[x]	3,4 Conj	
6.	(∃x)(Cx · ~Cx)	5 EG	

Our restriction rules this out by forbidding step 4. Each time FI is used, a new existential quasi-name must be introduced. Since "[x]" appeared earlier in the proof, a new quasi-name (for example "[y]") must be introduced here.

Exercise 7c

Using UI, EG, EI, NP, UN and UP, together with the rules of statement logic, prove that each is valid.

1. (∃x)(Fx · Gx)
    (∀x)(Gx ⊃ Hx)
    ———————————
    (∃x)(Fx · Hx)

2. (∃x)(Fx · Gx) ⊃ (Fa · Ja)
    (∃x)(Fx · Ex)
    (∀x)[Ex ⊃ (Gx · Hx)]
    (∀x)(Jx ⊃ Kx)
    ———————————
    (∃x)(Fx · Kx)

3. (∀x)(Ax ⊃ Bx)
    (∀x)(Bx ⊃ Cx)
    ———————————
    (∃x)(Ax) ⊃ (∃x)(Cx)

4. Ba · (∃x)(Bx · ~Fx)
    (∀x)(Bx ⊃ Ax)
    (Aa · Ca) ⊃ (∀x)[(Bx · ~Fx) ⊃ Gx]
    ———————————
    Ca ⊃ (∃x)[(Gx · ~Fx) · Ax]

5. Fa · Ga
    (∀x)[Gx ⊃ (Hx v ~Fx)]
    (∀x)[(Fx · Hx) ⊃ (∃y)(Rxy)]
    ———————————
    (∃x)(∃y)(Rxy)

6. (∃x)(∃y)[(Fx · Gy) · Rxy]
    (∀x)(Fx ⊃ Hx)
    (∀x)(Gx ⊃ Kx)
    ———————————
    (∃x)(∃y)[(Hx · Ky) · Rxy]

7. (∀x)(Fx ⊃ Gx)
    (∃x)(Fx · ~Ax)
    ———————————
    (∀y)(Dy ⊃ Ay) ⊃ (∃x)(Gx · ~Dx)

8. (∃x)(Fx · Gx)
    (∃y)(Fy · ~Gy)
    (x)(Gx ≡ Hx)
    ———————————
    (∃x)(Fx · Hx) · (∃y)(Fy · ~ Hy)

9. (∃x)(Fx · ~Gx)
    (∃x)(~Gx) ⊃ (∃y)(Hy · ~Gy)
    ———————————
    (∀x)(Hx ⊃ ~Fx) ⊃ (∃y)(~Gy · ~ Fy)

Proceed to the next section of the study guide.

UNIVERSAL GENERALIZATION

Our other major rule, universal generalization, will be used when we wish to prove something general.

| Universal | $\dfrac{Z(w)}{(\forall w)(Zw)}$ |
| Generalization | |

If we prove "Z(w)" (where "(w)" is a universal quasi-name), then we have proved that "Z" applies to any object that "(w)" might name. Thus, we may conclude that "(∀w)(Zw)" is true.

Restrictions

Universal generalization allows us to infer a universally quantified statement from the corresponding formula with a universal quasi-name. But there are two important restrictions that must be placed on uses of UG in order to prevent certain invalid inferences.

We must restrict our use of UG to formulas that contain no occurences of existential quasi-names. Otherwise, the following sequence would be allowed by our rules even though the last line does not follow from the first.

1.	(∀x)(∃y) Lxy		
2.	(∃y) L(x)y	1 UI	
3.	L(x) [y]	2 EI	
4.	(∀x) Lx [y]	3 UG	NOT PERMITTED
5.	(∃y)(∀x) Lxy	4 EG	

Line #1 says that everyone is a lover, but line #5 says that there is some individual who is universally loved (loved by everyone). Our system of rules should not allow such an inference. We prevent it by restricting UG so that line #4 is not allowed.

Another restriction on UG is related to the use of UU in proofs. We would be in trouble if we allowed ourselves to infer from the premise "Every basketball player is over six feet tall" the conclusion "If anyone is a basketball player, then everyone is over six feet tall". But as our rules stand now, we do not have a way to prevent this sequence:

1.	(∀x)(Bx ⊃ Cx)		
2.	B(x) ⊃ C(x)	1UI	
*3.	B(x)	ACP	
*4.	C(x)	2,3 MP	
*5.	C(y)	4 UU	
*6.	(∀y)(Cy)	5 UG	
7.	B(x) ⊃ (∀y)(Cy)	3-6 RCP	
8.	(∀x)[Bx ⊃ (∀y)(Cy)]	7 UG	NOT PERMITTED

If #1 says "Every basketball player is over six feet tall", then #8 say "If anyone is a basketball player, then everyone is over six feet tall" (in other words, "Pick any individual x; if x is a basketball player, then everyone is over six feet tall.") It may be true that all basketball players are over six feet tall. It is certainly not true that everyone is over six feet tall. So #1 may be true when #8 is false, and this derivation must be prohibited.

To make the statement of the necessary restriction on UG clear and succint, it is useful to introduce the notion of dependence.

A line m of a derivation <u>depends on</u> an earlier like k of that derivation if and only if

a) line m is derived from line k (possibly in combination with other lines) by one of the rules of inference

<u>OR</u>

b) there is a line l (between k and m) and line l depends on line k and line m depends on line l.

UG cannot be employed to derive "$(\forall x)(Zx)$" from "$Z(x)$" if "$Z(x)$" depends on a line derived by UU from a formula containing the universal quasi-name "(x)". The attempt to use UG in line #8 to derive "$(\forall x)[Bx \supset (\forall y)(Cy)]$" is incorrect. Line #8 depends upon line #5, and line #5 is derived by UU from a formula containing "(x)". (To see that line #8 depends upon line #5, trace back the justifications given on the right. Line #8 depends on line #7, and line #7 depends on #3-6. So line #8 depends - indirectly - on #3-6, and thus on #5.)

Our complete statement of UG should include these restrictions.

Universal
<u>Generalization</u>

$$\frac{Z(w)}{(\forall w)(Zw)}$$

This inference is allowed provided that
a) no existential quasi-name appears in $Z(w)$ <u>and</u>
b) $Z(w)$ does not depend on a line derived by $\overline{UU}$ from a formula containing "(w)".

Exercise 7d

Prove that each of these is valid. (Rules: UI, EG, EI, UG, UN, NP, UP, UU and the rules of statement logic.)

1. $(\forall x)[(Ax \lor Bx) \supset Cx]$
    $\underline{(\forall x)[(Cx \lor Dx) \supset Ex]}$
    $(\forall x)(Ax \supset Ex)$

2. $(\forall x)(Ax \supset Bx)$
    $\underline{(\exists x)(\sim Bx)}$
    $(\exists x)(\sim Ax)$

3. $(\forall x)(Bx \supset (\forall y)(Hy))$
    $Rc \supset Bc$
    $\underline{\sim Ib \supset Rc}$
    $\sim Ib \supset (\forall y)(Hy)$

4. $[(\exists y)(Sy) \cdot (\exists z)(Tz)] \supset Ma$
    $\underline{(\exists x)(Sx \cdot Tx)}$
    Ma

5. $(\exists x)(Ax) \supset (\exists y)(By)$
    $(\forall x)(Bx \supset Cx)$
    $\underline{(\forall x)(\sim Cx)}$
    $\sim(\exists x)(Ax)$

6. $(\forall x)[Ax \supset ((\exists y)(By) \supset Cx)]$
    $\underline{(\forall x)[Cx \supset ((\exists y)(Dy) \supset Ex)]}$
    $(\exists x)(Bx \cdot Dx) \supset (\forall y)(Ay \supset Ey)$

7. $(\exists x)(Ax \cdot Bx)$
    $(\forall x)(Cx \supset Dx)$
    $\underline{(\forall x)[Ax \supset ((\exists y)(Ey \cdot Dy) \supset Fx)]}$
    $(\exists x)(Cx \cdot Ex) \supset (\exists y)(Fy)$

8.* $(\exists x)(Ax \cdot \sim Bx)$
    $(\forall y)[(\exists x)(Ax \cdot Ryx) \supset (\exists z)(Bz \cdot Ryz)]$
    $\underline{(\forall x)[(Ax \cdot \sim Bx) \supset (\exists y)(Ryx)]}$
    $(\exists x)(Bx \cdot (\exists y)Ryx)$

Read the section of the text entitled "Exchange and Distribution Rules," then proceed to the next section of this study guide.

EXCHANGE RULES

The instantiation and generalization rules apply only to quantifiers governing statements that appear as complete lines of proof. They do not apply to negated quantified statements or to other truth-functional compounds of quantified statements.

What can we do with negated quantified statements if the instantiation and generalization rules do not apply? One thing, of course, is to use them in inferences involving only statement logic rules.

```
1.  ~(∃x)Fx
2.  (∃y)Gy ⊃ (∃x)Fx
3.  ~(∃y)Gy                    1,2 MT
```

This is a perfectly legitmate case of modus tollens.

Far more commonly, however, we shall want to use an instantiation rule to "get rid of" the quantifiers in such statements. To make this possible, we introduce the quantifier exchange equivalence rules.

Quantifier Exchange	$\dfrac{\sim(w)(Zw)}{(\exists w)\sim(Zw)}$	$\dfrac{\text{Not everything is Z}}{\text{Something is not Z}}$
	$\dfrac{\sim(\exists w)(Zw)}{(w)\sim(Zw)}$	$\dfrac{\text{Nothing is Z}}{\text{Everything is non-Z}}$
	$\dfrac{(w)(Zw)}{\sim(\exists w)\sim(Zw)}$	$\dfrac{\text{Everything is Z}}{\text{Nothing is non-Z}}$
	$\dfrac{(\exists w)(Zw)}{\sim(w)\sim(Zw)}$	$\dfrac{\text{Something is Z}}{\text{Not everything is non-Z}}$

In derivations, the most common use of these rules will be to "drive in" the negation sign in any premise that contains a quantifier preceded by a negation sign. In this respect these rules are like the DeMorgan's rules in statement logic, and they are often used together.

```
1.  ~(∃x)(Fx · Gx)
2.  (∀x)(~Hx v Fx)           (∀x)(~Hx v ~Gx) ?
3.  (∀x)~(Fx · Gx)           1 QE
4.  (∀x)(~Fx v ~Gx)          3 DEM
5.  ~H(x) v F(x)             2 UI
6.  ~F(x) v ~G(x)            4 UI
7.  ~H(x) v ~G(x)            5,6 CC
8.  (∀x)(~Hx v ~Gx)          7 UG
```

After the negation is driven in, as in step #4, instantiation is possible (step #5), thus eliminating the quantifier.

STRATEGY TIPS

In devising derivations, you will probably find it helpful to keep the following in mind.

1. Use QE (and DeM) to "drive in" negations appearing before quantifiers.
2. Use EI as soon as possible when you have an existential premise.
3. If the conclusion is a universally quantified conditional, it will almost always be derived by UG on a conditional. The conditional will usually be proved by RCP.
4. If the conclusion is of the form "(∃w)(Zw)" it will almost always be proved from "Z[w]". "Z[w]" may be derived from previous lines containing "[w]" or it may be derived from "Zn" where "n" is some name. Try to determine which name or quasi-name will be used in establishing "Z[w]".
5. A formula "Z(x)" with a universal quasi-name may be used together with other formulas containing "(x)". On the other hand, UN or UP may be used to replace "(x)" by a name or by an existential quasi-name. Try to determine which strategy is best. If "(x)" is to be replaced, determine what the most useful replacements will be.

<u>Exercise 7e</u>

Prove that each is valid.

1. ~(∃x)(Ax · Bx)
    (∀x)(Cx ⊃ Bx)
    ‾‾‾‾‾‾‾‾‾‾‾‾‾‾‾‾
    ~(∃x)(Ax · Cx)

2. ~(∀x)(Ax)
    (∀x)(~Ax ⊃ Bx)
    ‾‾‾‾‾‾‾‾‾‾‾‾‾‾‾‾
    (∃x)(Bx)

3. ~(∃x)(Ax)
    ~(∃x)(Bx · ~Ax)
    ‾‾‾‾‾‾‾‾‾‾‾‾‾‾‾‾
    ~(∃x)Bx

4. (∀x)(Ax ⊃ Fx)
    ~ (∃x)(Fx)
    ‾‾‾‾‾‾‾‾‾‾‾‾‾‾‾
    (∀x)(~Ax · ~Fx)

5. ~(∀x)(Ax ⊃ Bx)
    (∀x)(~Bx ⊃ ~(∃y)(Rxy))
    Ca
    ‾‾‾‾‾‾‾‾‾‾‾‾‾‾‾‾‾‾‾‾‾‾‾‾
    (∃x)(∃y)[(Ax · Cy) · ~Rxy]

6. (∃x)(Fx · Gx)
    (∀x)(Fx ⊃ Kx)
    (∃x)(Gx · Kx) ⊃ (∀x)(Gx ⊃ Hx)
    (∀x)(Hx ⊃ Jx)
    ‾‾‾‾‾‾‾‾‾‾‾‾‾‾‾‾‾‾‾‾‾‾‾‾‾‾‾‾‾‾‾‾
    ~(∀x)(Fx ⊃ ~Jx)

7. (∀z)[Gz ⊃ (∀y)(Fy ⊃ Lyz)]
    (∀x)[Fx ⊃ ~(∀y)(Lxy)]
    (∃x)(Gx)
    ‾‾‾‾‾‾‾‾‾‾‾‾‾‾‾‾‾‾‾‾‾‾‾‾‾‾‾‾‾‾‾
    (∀x)[Fx ⊃ ((∃y)(Lxy) · (∃z)(~Lxz))]

8. (∀x)(Ax ⊃ (∀y)(Ryx))
    ~(∃x)(∀y)(Ryx)
    ‾‾‾‾‾‾‾‾‾‾‾‾‾‾‾‾‾‾‾‾‾‾‾‾‾‾‾‾‾‾‾
    ~(∃x)(Ax) · (∀x)(∃y)(~Ryx)

9.* (∀x)(∀y)(Rxy ⊃ Ryx)
    Rab
    (∀x)[(∃y)(Rxy) ⊃ Rxx]
    (∃x)~(∃y)(Rxy)
    ‾‾‾‾‾‾‾‾‾‾‾‾‾‾‾‾‾‾‾‾‾‾‾‾‾‾‾‾‾‾‾
    [Rbb · (∃y)(~Rby)] · (∀z)(Rbz ⊃ Rzz)

10. ~(∃x)(Ax · Cx) · (∃x)(Ax)
    (∃x)(Fx · ~Gx)
    (∀x)(~Gx ⊃ ~(∃y)(Rxy))
    ‾‾‾‾‾‾‾‾‾‾‾‾‾‾‾‾‾‾‾‾‾‾‾‾‾‾‾‾
    (∃x)(∃y)[(Fx · ~Cy) · ~Rxy]

Proceed to the next section of the study guide.

<u>QUANTIFIER DISTRIBUTION</u>

Although the quantifier distribution rules are not required for our system (we could derive just as much without them), many proofs are simpler if we add them. In any case, they formulate inferences and equivalences that are worth noting.

<u>Quantifier
Distribution</u> $\dfrac{(\forall w)(Yw \cdot Zw)}{(\forall w)(Yw) \cdot (\forall w)(Zw)}$

$$\frac{(\exists w)(Yw \lor Zw)}{(\exists w)(Yw) \lor (\exists w)(Zw)}$$

$$\frac{(\forall w)(Yw) \lor (\forall w)(Zw)}{(\forall w)(Yw \lor Zw)}$$

$$\frac{(\exists w)(Yw \cdot Zw)}{(\exists w)(Yw) \cdot (\exists w)(Zw)}$$

Exercise 7f

Without consulting the text, explain why the last two QD rules are one-way rules. Do this by giving examples that show the <u>invalidity</u> of each of the following inferences.

$$\frac{(\forall x)(Fx \lor Gx)}{(\forall x)(Fx) \lor (\forall x)(Gx)} \qquad\qquad \frac{(\exists x)(Fx) \cdot (\exists x)(Gx)}{(\exists x)(Fx \cdot Gx)}$$

Exercise 7g

Prove that each is valid.

1. $(\forall x)(Ax \cdot Bx)$
    $\underline{(\forall x)(Ax) \supset (\forall x)(Cx)}$
    $(\forall x)(Bx \cdot Cx)$

2. $\underline{Fa \lor Ga}$
    $(\exists x)(Fx) \lor (\exists x)(Gx)$

3. $(\exists x)(\sim Fx \lor Gx)$
    $(\exists x)(\sim Fx) \supset (\forall x)(Hx)$
    $\underline{(\exists x)(Gx) \supset (\forall x)(Hx)}$
    $(\forall x)(Hx)$

4. $(\forall x)(Ax \cdot Bx)$
    $\underline{(\exists x)(Bx) \supset (\forall x)(Ex)}$
    $(\forall x)(Ax \cdot Ex)$

5. $(\exists x)(Fx \cdot Gx)$
    $\underline{(\forall x)(Fx) \supset \sim(\exists x)(Gx)}$
    $(\exists x)(\sim Fx)$

6. $(\exists x)(Ax \cdot (\forall y)(Rxy))$
    $\underline{(\exists x)(\forall y)(Rxy) \supset \sim(\forall x)(Ax)}$
    $(\exists x)(Ax) \cdot (\exists y)(\sim Ay)$

Exercise 7h

Symbolize each argument and show that it is valid.

1. An engine that is very heavy will not run a car efficiently unless it is very costly. An engine is unacceptable if it is very costly or it does not run a car efficiently. Thus any engine that is very heavy is unacceptable.
2. No engine without a mileage rating can be sold. Nothing gets a mileage rating without being examined for safe design. Thus every engine that can be sold has been examined for safe design.
3. Ostriches and rheas are powerful but flightless. Anything that is powerful or venomous is potentially dangerous and makes a poor pet. Thus ostriches make poor pets.
4. Any well-adapted bird that lacks the power of flight must have ancestors that gained an adequate compensatory advantage. But the only adequate compensatory advantage is large size. Since kiwis are well-adapted but flightless birds, they must have had large ancestors. (Wx # x is well-adapted, Bx # x is a bird, Fx # x flies, Gx # x has ancestors that gained an adequate compensator advantage, Lx # x has large ancestors, Kx # x is a kiwi).
5. If there are regions without native mammals, there must be non-mammals that have evolved to fill typically mammalian roles. Anything that evolves to fill typically mammalian roles will have many characteristics that are typical of mammals. So some non-mammals must have many characteristics

typical of mammals, since there are regions without native mammals.

ENTHYMEMES AGAIN

    In an ordinary presentation of an argument it is not necessary to state every premise and the conclusion. Context will indicate that premises have been omitted, and some premises can be taken for granted.   Consider

                John must like spicy food, because
                everyone from Texas likes spicy food.

The speaker needn't explicitly state the missing premise because context makes it obvious what the premise must be.

    Consider also

                Since Al is taller than Bill and Bill
                is taller than Charlie, Al must be
                taller than Charlie.

Symbolized, this is

            Tab
            Tbc   Tac ?

The needed information is something we all know about the relation "taller than" (though it is not so easy to state in idiomatic English). It is a transitive relation. In other words,

        $(\forall x)(\forall y)(\forall z)[(Txy \cdot Tyz) \supset Txz]$

If this premise is added to the others, the deduction becomes a simple one (though tedious).

Exercise 7i

Symbolize and prove valid. At least some are enthymemes.

    1. All of Bob's children are married. Al is Bob's son. So Al must be married
    2. Of Bob's children, only his daughters are married. Al is Bob's son. So Al must not be married.
    3. Al must be married, since all of Bob's sons are married.
    4. Everyone in the society is a linguist or a philosopher, and none of the linguists are here. So all of the people here must be philosophers.
    5. No one shorter than Smith can join the team. Smith is taller than Jones. Thus Jones cannot join the team.
    6. Any linguist receives a higher pay than Jones, but Jones receives a higher pay than some philosophers. Thus each linguist receives a higher pay than some philosophers.

Exercise 7j

    Use the notation of this chapter to symbolize the arguments of Exercises 5f, 5g, 5h and 6g. Then derive the conclusions (filling in missing premises or conclusion in the case of enthymemes).

86

Read the section in the text on predicate
quantification, and then read the next
section of the study guide.

PREDICATE QUANTIFICATION

Think of predicates as standing for properties an object may have. If we wish
to say that John Wayne and Mickey Rooney share some properties, we may write

$$(\exists F)(Fj \cdot Fm).$$

The quantificational rules can be extended in a natural way to provide for inferences
involving such predicate quantifications.

Do exercises 7A, 7B, 7C and 7D in the text.
Then read the section entitled "Identity" in
the text before proceding to the next section
of the study guide.

IDENTITY

Identity is a fundamental concept. Many common types of sentences involve
it, and several important inferences are characteristic of it.

Let us first consider some of the most common statements involving identity.

Exceptives

The words "everyone but n", "everyone else but n", "everyone other than n",
"no one but n" and "only n" indicated the need to exclude the individual denoted by
"n". The identity relation will be needed in the symbolization.

Everyone famous except Marlon Brando was at the banquet.
$(\forall x)[(Fx \cdot \sim(x=b)) \supset Bx]$

John Wayne is taller than everyone else.
$(\forall x)(\sim(x=j) \supset Tjx)$

Only John Wayne talks like that.
$(\forall x)(\sim(x=j) \supset \sim Tx)$
$(\forall x)(Tx \supset x=j)$

Superlatives

Superlative expressions "n is the best F" or "n is the best F that is G"
are closely related to comparative relations "x is a better F than y is". Representing these superlatives in terms of the corresponding comparative requires the
employment of the identity relation.

Marlon Brando is the best actor of all.
Bxy # x is a better actor than y
$(\forall x)(\sim(x=b) \supset Bbx)$

87

John Wayne is the best actor in the cast.
(∀x)[(Cx · ~(x=j)) ⊃ Bjx] · Cj

Numerical Concepts

Numerical concepts ("at least one", "at least two", etc., "at most one", "at most two", etc., "exactly one", "exactly two", etc.) can now be represented.

At least

There was at least one horse in the film
Hx # x is a horse
Fx # x was in the film
(∃x)(Hx · Fx)   (Identity relation not needed)

There were at least two horses in the film.
(∃x)(∃y)[~(x=y) · Hy · Fx · Fy]
(Identity relation needed)

There were at least three horses in the film.
(∃x)(∃y)(∃z)[~(x=y) · ~(y=z) · ~(x=z)
Hx · Hy · Hz · Fx · Fy · Fz]

At most

There was at most one horse in the film.
(There were not at last two.)
~(∃x)(∃y)[~(x=y) • Hx · Hy · Fx · Fy]
(∀x)(∀y)[(Hx · Fx · Hy · Fy) ⊃ x=y]
(These are equivalent.)

There were at most two horses in the film.
~(∃x)(∃y)(∃z)[~(x=y) · ~(y=z) · ~(x=z).
Hx · Hy · Hz · Fx · Fy · Fz]

OR

(∀x)(∀y)(∀z)[(Hx · Fx · Hy · Fy · Hz · Fz) ⊃ (x=y v x=z v y=z)]
(These are equivalent.)

Exactly

There was exactly one horse in the film.
(∃x)(Hx · Fx) · (∀x)(∀y)[(Hx · Fx · Hy · Fy) ⊃ y=x)]

OR

(∃x)[(Hx · Fx) · (∀y)((Hy · Fy) ⊃ y=x)]

There were exactly two horses in the film.
(∃x)(∃y)[(Hx · Fx · Hy · Fy) · (∀z)((Hz · Fz) ⊃ (z=x v z=y))]

Exercise 7k

Symbolize the following sentences.

1. Enstein knew more then anyone else.
   (Kxy # x knew more than y)

88

2. Only Einstein was capable of devising such a theory. (Cx # x was capable of devising such a theory)
3. Einstein knew more than any other physicist.
4. Einstein is the physicist who knew the most.
5. Einstein is not the physicist who knew the most.
6. There are at least two physicists who were capable of devising such a theory.
7. At most two physicists know more than Einstein.
8. Other than Einstein, there are at most two people who could have devised such a theory.
9. There are exactly two physicists who could have devised such a theory.
10. There are at least three physicists who knew more than Einstein and could have devised such a theory.

Now read the section of the text entitled
"Iota and Lambda Expressions," then proceed to the next section of the study guide.

DEFINITE DESCRIPTIONS

An English noun phrase formed by putting the word "the" before a predicative expression is a definite description.

The chairman gave out awards.

In using such a noun phrase to refer to a single individual one assumes that, within the limits of the conversational context, there is exactly one individual to whom the predicative expression applies. Thus the statement above can be represented.

$$Cx \text{ # } x \text{ is a chairman}$$
$$Gx \text{ # } x \text{ gave out awards}$$
$$(\exists x) [Cx \cdot (y)(Cy \supset y=x) \cdot Gx]$$

"There is exactly one chairman (who we might be talking about in this context) and he gave out awards."

Exercise 71

Symbolize the following sentences.

1. The physicist who devised this theory was a genius.
2. Jones knows the person who devised this theory.
3. Jones does not know the person who devised this theory, but the one who did it is more famous than anyone else.
4. The man who killed Jones killed himself.

Do Exercise 7E in the text, then proceed
to the next section of the study guide.

IDENTITY INFERENCES

To our deductive system we will add the following rules in order to make derivations involving identity possible.

Commutativity	$a=b$
(Com Id)	$b=a$

Transitivity	$a=b$
(Trans Id)	$b=c$
	$a=c$

Identity	$a=b$	$a=b$
(Id)	Za	Zb
	Zb	Za

Negation of Identity	Za
(Neg Id)	$\sim Zb$
	$\sim(a=b)$

Exercise 7m

Show that each is valid.

1. $(\forall y)(Fy \supset y=a)$
   Fb
   $b=a$

2. $\sim(b=c)$
   $(a=b) \supset \sim(a=c)$

3. $Fa \cdot \sim Fb$
   $(\forall x)(\sim(x=a) \supset Rax)$
   Rab

4. $(\forall x)(Fx \supset x=a)$
   $(\forall x)(Gx \supset x=b)$
   $(\exists x)(Fx \cdot Gx)$
   $a=b$

5. $(\forall x)[(Fx \cdot \sim(x=a)) \supset Rax]$
   $\sim Rab$
   Fb
   $b=a$

6. $(\exists x)[Fx \cdot (\forall y)(Fy \supset y=x)]$
   $(\forall x)(Gx \supset Fx) \cdot (\exists x)(Gx)$
   $(\exists x)[Gx \cdot (\forall y)(Gy \supset y=x)]$

7. $(\forall y)[(\exists x)(Px \cdot Ryx) \supset y=a]$
   $(\forall x)[Px \supset (\exists y)(\exists z)(\sim(y=z) \cdot Ryx \cdot Rzx)]$
   $\sim(\exists x)(Px)$

8. $\sim(\exists x)(Ax \cdot Bx)$
   $\sim Ac$
   $(\forall x)(\sim(x=c) \supset (Ax \supset Bx))$
   $\sim(\exists x)(Ax)$

9.* $(\exists x)[Qx \cdot (\forall y)(Py \supset y=x) \cdot (\forall y)(\sim(y=x) \supset Rxy)]$
   $(\forall x)[Px \supset (\forall y)(\sim Qy \supset Rxy)]$

10.* $(\forall x)(Px \supset Qx)$
   $(\exists x)[Px \cdot (\forall y)(Ry \supset x=y)]$
   $\sim(\forall x)(Rx \supset Sx)$
   $(\exists x)[(Rx \cdot (\forall y)(Ry \supset x=y)) \cdot (Qx \cdot \sim Sx)]$

Now do Exercise 7F in the text.

Exercise 7n*

Symbolize each and prove that it is valid.

1. The hardest problem on the exam was not solved by anyone. No one will get an A without solving every problem on the exam. So no one will get an A.
2. No plan can pass. This is because only plans that meet student needs can pass. But no plan designed by a faculty committee will meet student needs, and only a plan designed by a faculty committee can pass.

3. No one at this meeting except Jones was at the convention. Mr. X was at the convention, murdered Baker there, and signed up to attend this meeting. Everyone who signed up to attend this meeting is here. So it must be Jones who murdered Baker.

4. Some committee members are on the faculty and some are not. One faculty-member on the committee is a scientist and two are not. Thus there are at least four committee members.

5. Only Smith knows as much as Adams. Smith and Adams are in the philosophy department and Jones is not. So there is someone who is not in the philosophy department who does not know as much as Adams.

6. Only one chemist is also a biologist, and she is a Nobel Prize winner. There is a chemist who is both a biologist and a musician. Thus there is a Nobel Prize winner who is also a musician.

7. Al was the only one who would profit from a deal. But no one enters a deal unless he will profit from it, and it takes two to make a deal. So there was no deal.

7a

i.
1. (∀x)(Tx ⊃ Sx)
3. ~(∀x)(Tx ⊃ Sx)   OR   (∃x)(Tx · ~Sx)
5. (∃x)[Tx · (Sx · Cx)]
7. ~(∃x)[(Tx · Sx) · Cx] OR (∀x)[(Tx · Sx) ⊃ ~Cx]
9. (∃x)(Kxa)
11. (∀x)(Kax ⊃ Sx)
13. Kaa
14. (∃x)(Kxx)

ii.
1. (∀x)(Ex ⊃ Mx)
3. (∀x)(Ex ⊃ Mx)
5. (∀x)(Ex ⊃ Mx)
7. (∀x)(Mx ⊃ Ex)   OR   (∀x)(~Ex ⊃ ~Mx)
9. (∃x)(Fx · ~Mx)
11. (∃x)(Fx · Mx) · (∃x)(Fx · Px)
13. Pe · Se
15. (∀x)[(Px v Fx) ⊃ Dx]   OR   (∀x)(Px ⊃ Dx) · (∀x)(Fx ⊃ Dx)
17. (∃x)[Fx · (Px · Mx)]
19. (∀x)(Fx ⊃ Kbx)
21. (∀x)(∃y)(Kxy)
23. (∀x)[Px ⊃ (∃y)(Fy · Kxy)]
25. (∃x)[(Ax · Fx) · (∀y)(Py ⊃ Kxy) · (∀y)(My ⊃ Kxy)]

7b
1.
1. (∀x)(Ax ⊃ Bx)
2. (∀x)(Bx ⊃ Cx)
3. ~Ca
4. A(x) ⊃ B(x)   1 UI
5. B(x) ⊃ C(x)   2 UI
6. Aa ⊃ Ba   4 UN
7. Ba ⊃ Ca   5 UN
8. ~Ba   3,7 MT
9. ~Aa   6,8 MT

3.
1. Fb · Gb
2. (∀x)(Gx ⊃ Rx)
3. (∀x)[(Rx · Fx) ⊃ Mx]
4. G(x) ⊃ R(x)   2 UI
5. Gb ⊃ Rb   4 UN
6. Gb   1 Simp
7. Rb   5,6 MP
8. (R(x) · F(x)) ⊃ M(x)   3 UI
9. (Rb · Fb) ⊃ Mb   8 UN
10. Fb   1 Simp
11. Rb · Fb   7, 10 Conj
12. Mb   9,11 MP
13. M[x]   12 NP
14. (∃x)(Mx)   13 EG

5.
1. Fa · Fb
2. (∀x)(Fx ⊃ Dx)
3. (Da · Ea) ⊃ Gb
*4. Ea   ACP
*5. Fa   1 Simp
*6. F(x) ⊃ D(x)   2 UI
*7. Fa ⊃ Da   6 UN
*8. Da   5,7 MP
*9. Da · Ea   4,8 Conj
*10. Gb   3,9 MP
*11. Fb ⊃ Db   6 UN
*12. Fb   1 Simp
*13. Db   11,12 MP
*14. Db · Gb   10,13 Conj
*15. D[x] · G[x]   14 NP
*16. (∃x)(Dx · Gx) 15 EG
17. Ea ⊃ (∃x)(Dx · Gx) 4-16 RCP

7.   1.   Rab
     2.   (∀x)(Rxb ⊃ Rx)
     3.   ~Fb
     4.   R(x)b ⊃ F(x)   2 UI
     5.   Rab ⊃ Fa   4 UN
     6.   Fa   1,5 MP
     7.   F[x]   6 NP
     8.   (∃x)(Fx)   7 EG
     9.   ~F[y]   3 NP
  10.   (∃y)(~Fy)   9 EG
  11.   (∃x)(Fx) · (∃y)(~Fy)   8,10 Conj

9.   1.   (∀x)(Fx ⊃ Gx)
     2.   (∀x)(∀y)[(~Fx · Gy) ⊃ Rxy]
     3.   (∀x)(Hx ⊃ ~Gx)
     4.   Ha · Fb
     5.   (∀y)[(~F(x) · Gy) ⊃ R(x)y]   2 UI
     6.   (~F(x) · G(y)) ⊃ R(x)(y)   5 UI
     7.   (~Fa · G(y)) ⊃ Ra(y)   6 UN
     8.   (~Fa · Gb) ⊃ Rab   7 UN
     9.   H(x) ⊃ ~G(x)   3 UI
  10.   Ha ⊃ ~Ga   9 UN
  11.   Ha   4 Simp
  12.   ~Ga   10,11 MP
  13.   F(x) ⊃ G(x)   1 UI
  14.   Fa ⊃ Ga   13 UN
  15.   ~Fa   12,14 MP
  16.   Fb ⊃ Gb   13 UN
  17.   Fb   4 Simp
  18.   Gb   16,17 MP
  19.   ~Fa · Gb   15,18 Conj
  20.   Rab   8,19 MP
  21.   Hb ⊃ ~Gb   9 UN
  22.   ~~Gb   18 DN
  23.   ~Hb   21,22 MI
  24.   ~Hb · Rab   23,20 Conj
  25.   ~H[x] · Ra[x]   24 MJ
  26.   (∃x)(~Hx · Rax)   25 EG

7c

1.   1.   (∃x)(Fx · Gx)
     2.   (∀x)(Gx ⊃ Hx)
     3.   F[x] · G[x]   1 EI
     4.   G(x) ⊃ H(x)   2 UI
     5.   G[x] ⊃ H[x]   4 UP
     6.   G[x]   3 Simp
     7.   H[x]   5,6 MP
     8.   F[x]   3 Simp
     9.   F[x] · H[x]   7,8 Conj
  10.   (∃x)(Fx · Hx)   9 EG

3.   1.   (∀x)(Ax ⊃ Bx)
      2.   (∀x)(Bx ⊃ Cx)
  *3.   (∃x)(Ax)   ACP
  *4.   A[x]   3 UI
  *5.   A(x) ⊃ B(x)   1 UI
  *6.   B(x) ⊃ C(x)   2 UI
  *7.   A(x) ⊃ C(x)   5,6 HS
  *8.   A[x] ⊃ C[x]   7 UP
  *9.   C[x]   4,8 MP
 *10.   (∃x)(Cx)   9 EG

11.   (∃x)(Ax) ⊃ (∃x)(Cx)   3-10 RCP

5.   1.   Fa · Ga
     2.   (∀x)[Gx ⊃ (Hx v ~Fx)]
     3.   (∀x)[(Fx · Hx) ⊃ (∃y)(Rxy)]
     4.   G(x) ⊃ (H(x) v ~F(x))   2 UI
     5.   Ga ⊃ (Ha v ~Fa)   4 UN
     6.   Ga   1 Simp
     7.   Ha v ~Fa   5,6 MP
     8.   Fa   1 Simp
     9.   Ha   7,8 SC
   10.   Fa · Ha   8,9 Conj
   11.   (F(x) · H(x)) ⊃ (∃y)(R(x)y)   3 UI
   12.   (Fa · Ha) ⊃ (∃y)(Ray)   11 UN
   13.   (∃y)(Ray)   10,12 MP
   14.   (∃y)(R[x]y)   13 MP
   15.   (∃x)(∃y)(Rxy)   14 EG

7.   1.   (∀x)(Fx ⊃ Gx)
     2.   (∃x)(Fx · ~Ax)
  *3.   (∀y)(Dy ⊃ Ay)   ACP
  *4.   D(y) ⊃ A(y)   3 UI
  *5.   F[x] · ~A[x]   2 EI
  *6.   ~A[x]   5 Simp
  *7.   D[x] ⊃ A[x]   4 UP
  *8.   ~D[x]   6,7 MP
  *9.   F[x]   5 Simp
 *10.   F(x) ⊃ G(x)   1 UI
 *11.   F[x] ⊃ G[x]   10 UP 9, 11 MP
 *12.   G[x]   9,11 MP
 *13.   G[x] · ~D[x]   8,12 Conj
 *14.   (∃x)(Gx · ~Dx)   13 EG
  15.   (∀y)(Dy ⊃ Ay) ⊃ (∃x)(Gx · ~Dx)   3-14 RCP

9.   1.   (∃x)(Fx · ~Gx)
     2.   (∃x)(~Gx) ⊃ (∃y)(Hy · ~Gy)
  *3.   (∀x)(Hx ⊃ ~Fx)   ACP
  *4.   F[x] · ~G[x]   1 EI
  *5.   ~G[x]   4 Simp
  *6.   (∃x)(~Gx)   5 EG
  *7.   (∃y)(Hy · ~Gy)   2,6 MP
  *8.   H[y] · ~G[y]   7 EI
  *9.   H(x) ⊃ ~F(x)   3 UI
 *10.   H[y] ⊃ ~F[y]   9 UP
 *11.   H[y]   8 Simp
 *12.   ~F[y]   10,11 MP
 *13.   ~G[y]   8 Simp
 *14.   ~G[y] · ~F[y]   12,13 Conj
 *15.   (∃y)(~Gy · ~Fy)   14 EG
  16.   (∀x)(Hx ⊃ ~Fx) ⊃ (∃y)(~Gy · ~Fy)   3-15 RCP

7d
1.   1.   (∀x[(Ax v Bx) ⊃ Cx]
     2.   (∀x)[(Cx v Dx) ⊃ Ex]
     3.   (A(x) v B(x)) ⊃ C(x)   1 UI
     4.   (C(x) v D(x)) ⊃ E(x)   2 UI
  *5.   A(x)   ACP
  *6.   A(x) v B(x)   5 Add
  *7.   C(x)   3,6 MP
  *8.   C(x) v D(x)   7 Add
  *9.   E(x)   7,8 MP
  10.   A(x) ⊃ E(x)   5-9 RCP
  11.   (∀x)(Ax ⊃ Ex)   10 UG

3. 1.   (∀x)(Bx ⊃ (∀y)(Hy))
    2.   Rc ⊃ Bc
    3.   ~Ib ⊃ Rc
   *4.   ~Ib   ACP
   *5.   Rc   3,4 MP
   *6.   Bc   2,5 MP
   *7.   B(x) ⊃ (∀y)(Hy)   1 UI
   *8.   Bc ⊃ (∀y)(Hy)   7 UN
   *9.   (∀y)(Hy)   6,8 MP
   10.   ~Ib ⊃ (∀y)(Hy)   4-9 CP

5. 1.   (∃x)(Ax) ⊃ (∃y)(By)
    2.   (∀x)(Bx ⊃ Cx)
    3.   (∀x)(~Cx)
    4.   ~C(x)   3 UI
    5.   B(x) ⊃ C(x)   2 UI
    6.   ~B(x)   4,5 MT
    7.   ~B(y)   6 UU
    8.   (∀y)(~By)   7 UG
    9.   ~(∃y)(By)   8 QE
   10.   ~(∃x)(Ax)   1,9 MT

7. 1.   (∃x)(Ax · Bx)
    2.   (∀x)(Cx ⊃ Dx)
    3.   (∀x)[Ax ⊃ ((∃y)(Ey · Dy) ⊃ Fx)]
   *4.   (∃x)(Cx · Ex)   ACP
   *5.   A[x] · B[x]   1 EI
   *6.   C[y] · E[y]   4 EI
   *7.   A(x) ⊃ ((∃y)(Ey · Dy) ⊃ F(x))   3 EI
   *8.   A[x] ⊃ ((∃y)(Ey · Dy) ⊃ F[x]) 7 UP
   *9.   A[x]   5 Simp
  *10.   (∃y)(Ey · Dy) ⊃ F[x]   8,9 MP
  *11.   C[y]   6 Simp
  *12.   C(x) ⊃ D(x)   2 UI
  *13.   C[y] ⊃ D[y]   12 UP
  *14.   D[y]   11,13 MP
  *15.   E[y]   6 Simp
  *16.   E[y] · D[y]   14,15 Conj
  *17.   (∃y)(Ey · Dy)   16 EG
  *18.   F[x]   10,17 MP
  *19.   (∃y)(Fy)   18 EG
   20.   (∃x)(Cx · Ex) ⊃ (∃y)(Fy)   4-19 RCP

7e
1. 1.   ~(∃x)(Ax · B(x))
    2.   (∀x)(Cx ⊃ Bx)
    3.   (∀x)[~(Ax · Bx)]   1 QE
    4.   ~(A(x) · B(x))   3 UI
    5.   ~A(x) v ~B(x)   4 DeM
    6.   C(x) ⊃ B(x)   2 UI
    7.   ~C(x) v B(x)   6 DMI
    8.   ~A(x) v ~C(x)   5,7 CC
    9.   ~(A(x) · C(x))   8 DeM
   10.   (∀x)[~(Ax · Cx)]   9 UG
   11.   ~(∃x)(Ax · Cx)   10 QE

3. 1.   ~(∃x)(Ax)
    2.   ~(∃x)(Bx · ~Ax)
    3.   (∀x)(~Ax)   1 QE
    4.   (∀x) ~(Bx · ~Ax)   2 QE
    5.   ~A(x)   3 UI

95

```
      6.   ~(B(x) · ~A(x))                          4 UI
      7.   ~B(x) v ~~·A(x)                           6 DeM
      8.   ~B(x)                                     5,7 SC
      9.   (∀x)(~Bx)                                 8 UG
     10.   ~(∃x)(Bx)                                 9 QE


5.   1.   ~(∀x)(Ax ⊃ Bx)
     2.   (∀x)(~Bx ⊃ ~(∃y)(Rxy))
     3.   Ca
     4.   (∃x)[~(Ax ⊃ Bx)]                           1 QE
     5.   ~(A[x] ⊃ B[x])                             4 EI
     6.   ~(~A[x] v B[x])                            5 DMI
     7.   ~~A[x] · ~B[x]                             6 DeM
     8.   ~B[x]                                      7 Simp
     9.   ~B(x) ⊃ ~(∃y)(R(x)y)                       2 UI
    10.   ~B[x] ⊃ ~(∃y)(R[x]y)                       9 UP
    11.   ~(∃y)(R[x]y)                               8,10 MP
    12.   (∀y)(~R[x]y)                               11 QE
    13.   ~R[x](y)                                   12 UI
    14.   ~R[x]a                                     13 UN
    15.   ~~A[x]                                     7 Simp
    16.   A[x]                                       15 DN
    17.   A[x] · Ca                                  3,16 Conj
    18.   (A[x] · Ca) · ~R[x]a                       17,14 Conj
    19.   (A[x] · C[y]) · ~R[x][y]                   18 NP
    20.   (∃y)[(A[x] · Cy) · ~R[x]y]                 19 EG
    21.   (∃x)(∃y)[(Ax · Cy) · ~Rxy]                 20 EG


7.   1.   (∀z)[Gz ⊃ (∀y)(Fy ⊃ Lyz)]
     2.   (∀x)[Fx ⊃ ~(∀z)(Lxz)]
     3.   (∃x)(Gx)
    *4.   F(x)                                       ACP
    *5.   F(x) ⊃ ~(∀z)(L(x)z)                        2 UI
    *6.   ~(∀z)(L(x)z)                               4,5 MP
    *7.   (∃z)(~L(x)z)                               6 QE
    *8.   ~L(x)[y]                                   7 EI
    *9.   G[z]                                       3 EI
   *10.   G(z) ⊃ (∀y)(Fy ⊃ Ly(z))                    1 UI
   *11.   G[z] ⊃ (∀y)(Fy ⊃ Ly[z])                    10 UP
   *12.   (∀y)(Fy ⊃ Ly[z])                           9,11 MP
   *13.   F(y) ⊃ L(y)[z]                             12 UI
   *14.   F(x) ⊃ L(x)[z]                             13 UU
   *15.   L(x)[z]                                    4,14 MP
   *16.   (∃y)(L(x)y)                                15 EG
   *17.   (∃z)(~L(x)z)                               8 EG
   *18.   (∃y)(L(x)y) · (∃z)(~L(x)z)                 16,17 Conj
    19.   F(x) ⊃ ((∃y)(L(x)y) · (∃z)(~L(x)z))        4-18 RCP
    20.   (∀)[Fx ⊃ ((∃y)(Lxy) · (∃z)(~Lxz))]         19 UG


9.   1.   (∀x)(∀y)(Rxy ⊃ Ryx)
     2.   Rab
     3.   (∀x)[(∃y)(Rxy) ⊃ Rxx]
     4.   (∃x)~(∃y)(Rxy)
     5.   (∀y)(R(x)y ⊃ Ry(x))                        1 UI
     6.   R(x)(y) ⊃ R(y)(x)                          5 UI
     7.   (∃y)(R(x)y) ⊃ R(x)(x)                      3 UI
    *8.   Rb(z)                                      ACP
    *9.   Rb(y) ⊃ R(y)b                              6 UN
   *10.   Rb(z) ⊃ R(z)b                              9 UU
   *11.   R(z)b                                      8,10 MP
   *12.   R(z)[y]                                    11 NP
   *13.   (∃y)(R(z)y)                                12 EG
```

96

*14.	$(\exists y)(R(z)y) \supset R(z)(z)$	7 UU
*15.	$R(z)(z)$	13,14 MP
16.	$Rb(z) \supset R(z)(z)$	8-15 RCP
17.	$(\forall z)((Rbz \supset Rzz)$	16 UG
18.	$Ra(y) \supset R(y)a$	6 UN
19.	$Rab \supset Rba$	18 UN
20.	Rba	2,19 MP
21.	$Rb[y]$	20 NP
22.	$(\exists y)(Rby)$	21 EG
23.	$(\exists y)(Rby) \supset Rbb$	7 UN
24.	Rbb	22,23 MP
25.	$\sim(\exists y)(R[x]y)$	3 EI
26.	$(\forall y)\sim(R[x]y)$	25 QE
27.	$\sim R[x](y)$	26 UI
28.	$\sim R[x]b$	27 UN
29.	$Rb(y) \supset R(y)b$	6 UN
30.	$Rb(x) \supset R(x)b$	29 UU
31.	$Rb[x] \supset R[x]b$	30 UP
32.	$\sim Rb[x]$	28,31 MT
33.	$(\exists y)(\sim Rby)$	32 EG
34.	$Rbb \cdot (\exists y)(\sim Rby)$	24,33 Conj
35.	$(Rbb \cdot (\exists y)(\sim Rby)) \cdot (\forall z)(Rbz \supset Rzz)$	34,17 Conj

7g

1.
1.	$(\forall x)(Ax \cdot Bx)$	
2.	$(\forall x)(Ax) \supset (\forall x)(Cx)$	
3.	$(\forall x)(Ax) \cdot (\forall x)(Bx)$	1 QD
4.	$(\forall x)(Ax)$	3 Simp
5.	$(\forall x)(Cx)$	2,4 MP
6.	$(\forall x)(Bx)$	3 Simp
7.	$(\forall x)(Bx) \cdot (\forall x)(Cx)$	5,6 Conj
8.	$(\forall x)(Bx \cdot Cx)$	7 QD

3.
1.	$(\exists x)(\sim Fx \lor Gx)$	
2.	$(\exists x)(\sim Fx) \supset (\forall x)(Hx)$	
3.	$(\exists x)(Gx) \supset (\forall x)(Hx)$	
4.	$(\exists x)(\sim Fx) \lor (\exists x)(Gx)$	1 QD
5.	$(\forall x)(Hx) \lor (\forall x)(Hx)$	2,3,4 CD
6.	$(\forall x)(Hx)$	5 Rep

5.
1.	$(\exists x)(Fx \cdot Gx)$	
2.	$(\forall x)(Fx) \supset \sim(\exists x)(Gx)$	
3.	$(\exists x)(Fx) \cdot (\exists x)(Gx)$	1 QD
4.	$(\exists x)(Gx)$	3 Simp
5.	$\sim\sim(\exists x)(Gx)$	4 DN
6.	$\sim(\forall x)(Fx)$	2,5 MT
7.	$(\exists x)(\sim Fx)$	6 QE

7h

1.
1.	$(\forall x)[Hx \supset (\sim Cx \supset \sim Rx)]$	$(\forall x)(Hx \supset \sim Ax)?$
2.	$(\forall x)[(Cx \lor \sim Rx) \supset \sim Ax]$	
*3.	$H(x)$	ACP
*4.	$H(x) \supset (\sim C(x) \supset \sim R(x))$	1 UI
*5.	$\sim C(x) \supset \sim R(x)$	3,4 MP
*6.	$(C(x) \lor \sim R(x)) \supset \sim A(x)$	2 UI
*7.	$\sim\sim C(x) \lor \sim R(x)$	5 DMI
*8.	$C(x) \lor \sim R(x)$	7 DN
*9.	$\sim A(x)$	6,8 MP
*10.	$H(x) \supset \sim A(x)$	3-9 RCP
11.	$(\forall x)(Hx \supset \sim Ax)$	10 UG

3. 1.   (∀x)[(Ox v Rx) ⊃ (Px · Fx)]   (∀x)(Ox ⊃ Mx)?
    2.   (∀x)[(Px v Vx) ⊃ (Dx · Mx)]
   *3.   O(x)   ACP
   *4.   O(x) v R(x)   3 Add
   *5.   (O(x) v R(x)) ⊃ (P(x) · F(x))   1 UI
   *6.   P(x) · F(x)   4,5 MP
   *7.   P(x)   6 Simp
   *8.   P(x) v V(x)   7 Add
   *9.   (P(x) v V(x)) ⊃ (D(x) · M(x))   2 UI
  *10.   D(x) · M(x)   8,9 MP
  *11.   M(x)   10 Simp
   12.   O(x) ⊃ M(x)   3-11 Rcp
   13.   (∀x)(Ox ⊃ Mx)   12 UG

5. 1.   (∃x)(Rx) ⊃ (∃y)(∼My · Fy)
    2.   (∀x)(Fx ⊃ Cx)   (∃x)(∼Mx · Cx)?
    3.   (∃x)(Rx)   1,3 MP
    4.   (∃y)(∼My · Fy)   4 EI
    5.   ∼M[x] · F[x]   2 UI
    6.   F(x) ⊃ C(x)   6 UP
    7.   F[x] ⊃ C[x]   5 Simp
    8.   F[x]   7,8 MP
    9.   C[x]   5 Simp
   10.   ∼M[x]   9,10 Conj
   11.   ∼M[x] · C[x]   11 EG
   12.   (∃x)(∼Mx · Cx)

7i
1. 1.   (∀x)(Cxb ⊃ Mx)
    2.   Sab   Ma?
    3.   (∀x)(∀y)(Sxy ⊃ Cxy)   Missing
    4.   (∀y)(S(x)y ⊃ C(x)y)   3 UI
    5.   S(x)(y) ⊃ C(x)(y)   4 UI
    6.   Sa(y) ⊃ Ca(y)   5 UN
    7.   Sab ⊃ Cab   6 UN
    8.   Cab   2,7 MP
    9.   C(x)b ⊃ M(x)   1 UI
   10.   Cab ⊃ Ma   9 UN
   11.   Ma   8,10 MP

3. 1.   (∀x)(Sxb ⊃ Mx)   Ma?
    2.   Sab
    3.   S(x)b ⊃ M(x)   Missing
    4.   Sab ⊃ Ma   1 UI
    5.   Ma   3 UN
                                                 2,4 MD

5. 1.   (∀x)(Sxs ⊃ ∼Jx)
    2.   Tsj   Jj?
    3.   (∀x)(∀y)(Txy ⊃ Syx)   Missing
    4.   (∀y)(T(x)y ⊃ Sy(x))   3 UI
    5.   T(x)(y) ⊃ S(y)(x)   4 UI
    6.   Ts(y) ⊃ S(y)s   5 UN
    7.   Tsj ⊃ Sjs   6 UN
    8.   Sjs   2,7 MP
    9.   S(x)s ⊃ ∼J(x)   1 UI
   10.   Sjs ⊃ ∼Ji   9 UN
   11.   ∼Ji   8,10 MP

7k

1. (∀x)(x≠e ⊃ Kex)
3. (∀x)[(Px · x≠e) ⊃ Kex
5. ~(∀x)[(Px · x≠e) ⊃ Kex]   OR   (∃x)(Px · K̄xe)
7. (∀x)(∀y)(∀z)[(Kxe · Kye · Kze · Px · Py · Pz) ⊃ (x=y v x=z v y=z)]
9. (∃x)(∃y)[(Px · Py · Cx · Cy) · (∀z)((Pz · Cz) ⊃ (z=x v z=y))]

7l

1. (∃x)[(Px · Dx) · (∀y)((Py · Dy) ⊃ y=x) · Gx]   OR   G(↱x)(Px · Dx)
3. (∃x)[Dx · (∀y)(Dy ⊃ y=x) · ~Kjx · (∀y)(~(y=x) ⊃ F̄xy)]

7m
1. 1. (∀y)(Fy ⊃ y=a)
    2. Fb
    3. F(y) ⊃ (y)=a   1 UI
    4. Fb ⊃ b=a   3 UN
    5. b=a   2,4 MP

3. 1. Fa · ~Fb
    2. (∀x)(~(x=a) ⊃ Rax)
   *3. ~Rab   ACP
   *4. ~((x)=a) ⊃ Ra(x)   2 UI
   *5. ~(b=a) ⊃ Rab   4 UN
   *6. ~~(b=a)   3,5 MP
   *7. b=a   6 DN
   *8. Fa   1 Simp
   *9. Fb   7,8 ID
   10. ~Rab ⊃ Fb   3-9 RCP
   11. ~Fb   1 Simp
   12. ~~Rab   10,11 MT
   13. Rab   12 DN

5. 1. (∀x)[(Fx · ~(x=a)) ⊃ Rax]
    2. ~Rab
    3. Fb
    4. (F(x) · ~((x)=a)) ⊃ Ra(x)   1 UI
    5. (Fb · ~(b=a)) ⊃ Rab   4 UN
    6. ~(Fb · ~(b=a)   2,5 MT
    7. ~Fb v ~~(b=a)   6 DeM
    8. ~~(b=a)   3,7 SC
    9. b=a   8 DN

7. 1. (∀y)[(∃x)(Px · Rxy) ⊃ y=a]
    2. (∀x)[Px ⊃ (∃y)(∃z)(~(y=z) · Ryx · Rzx)]
   *3. (∃x)(Px)   ACP
   *4. P[x]   3 EI
   *5. P(x) ⊃ (∃y)(∃z)(~(y=z) · Ry(x) · Rz(x))   2 UI
   *6. P[x] ⊃ (∃y)(∃z)(~(y=z) · Ry[x] · Rz[x])   5 UP
   *7. (∃y)(∃z)(~(y=z) · Ry[x] · Rz[x])   4,6 MP
   *8. (∃z)(~([y]=z) · R[y][x] · Rz[x])   7 EI
   *9. ~([y]=[z]) · R[y][x] · R[z][x]   8 EI
  *10. (∃x)(Px · R(y)x) ⊃ (y)=a   1 UI
  *11. (∃x)(Px · R[y]x) ⊃ [y]=a   10 UP
  *12. R[y][x]   9 Simp
  *13. P[x] · R[y][x]   4,12 Conj
  *14. (∃x)(Px · R[y]x)   13 EG
  *15. [y]=a   11,14 MP
  *16. (∃x)(Px · R(z)x) ⊃ (z)=a   10 UU
  *17. (∃x)(Px · R[z]x) ⊃ [z]=a   16 UP

```
*18.   R[z][x]                                              9 Simp
*19.   P[x]  ·  R[z][x]                                     4,18 Conj
*20.   (∃x)(Px  ·  R[z]x)                                   19 EG
*21.   [z]=a                                                17,20 MP
*22.   a=[z]                                                21 Com ID
*23.   [y]=[z]                                              15,22 Trans ID
*24.   ~([y]=[z])                                           9 Simp
*25.   [y]=[z] v ~(∃x)(Px)                                  23 Add
*26.   ~(∃x)(Px)                                            24,25 SC
 27.   (∃x)(Px) ⊃ ~(∃x)(Px)                                 3-26 RCP
 28.   ~(∃x)(Px) v ~(∃x)(Px)                                27 DMI
 29.   ~(∃x)(Px)                                            28 REP


9.  1.   (∃x)[Qx · (∀y)(Py ⊃ y=x) · (∀y)(~(y=x) ⊃ Rxy)]
   *2.   P(z)                                               ACP
  **3.   ~Q(y)                                              ACP
  **4.   Q[x] · (∀y)(Py ⊃ y=[x]) · (∀y)(~(y=[x]) ⊃ R[x]y)   1 EI
  **5.   Q[x]                                               4 Simp
  **6.   ~([x]=(y))                                         3,5 Neg ID
  **7.   ~((y)=[x])                                         6 Comm ID
  **8.   (∀y)(~(y=[x]) ⊃ R[x]y)                             4 Simp
  **9.   ~((y)=[x]) ⊃ R[x](y)                               8 UI
 **10.   R[x](y)                                            7,9 MP
 **11.   (∀y)(Py ⊃ y=[x])                                   4 Simp
 **12.   P(y) ⊃ (y)=[x])                                    11 UI
 **13.   P(z) ⊃ (z) = [x]                                   12 UU
 **14.   (z)=[x]                                            2,13 MP
 **15.   R(z)(y)                                            10,14 ID
  *16.   ~Q(y) ⊃ R(z)(y)                                    3-15 RCP
  *17.   (∀y)(~Qy ⊃ R(z)y)                                  16 UG
   18.   P(z) ⊃ (∀y)(~Qy ⊃ R(z)y)                           2-17 RCP
   19.   P(x) ⊃ (∀y)(~Qy ⊃ R(x)y)                           18 UU
   20.   (∀x)[Px ⊃ (∀y)(~Qy ⊃ Rxy)]                         19 UG


7n
1.  1.   (∃x)(Ex · (∀y)[(Ey · ~(y=x)) ⊃ Hxy] · ~(∃z)(Szx))  (∃x)(Ax)?
    2.   (∀x)(Ax ⊃ (∀y)(Ey ⊃ Sxy))
   *3.   (∃x)(Ax)                                           ACP
   *4.   A[x]                                               3 EI
   *5.   A(x) ⊃ (∀y)(Ey ⊃ S(x)y)                            2 UI
   *6.   A[x] ⊃ (∀y)(Ey ⊃ S[x]y)                            5 UP
   *7.   (∀y)(Ey ⊃ S[x]y)                                   4,6 MP
   *8.   E[u] · (∀y)[(Ey · ~(y=[u])) ⊃ H[u]y] · ~(∃z)(Sz[u]) 1 EI
   *9.   E(y) ⊃ S[x](y)                                     7 UI
  *10.   E(u) ⊃ S[x](u)                                     9 UU
  *11.   E[u] ⊃ S[x][u]                                     10 UP
  *12.   E[u]                                               8 Simp
  *13.   S[x][u]                                            10,11 MP
  *14.   ~(∃z)(Sz[u])                                       8 Simp
  *15.   (∀z)(~Sz[u])                                       14 QE
  *16.   ~S(z)[u]                                           15 UI
  *17.   ~S(x)[u]                                           16 UU
  *18.   ~S[x][u]                                           17 UP
  *19.   S[x][u] v ~(∃x)(Ax)                                13 Add
  *20.   ~(∃x)(Ax)                                          18,19 SC
   21.   (∃x)(Ax) ⊃ ~(∃x)(Ax)                               3-21 RCP
   22.   ~(∃x)(Ax) v ~(∃x)(Ax)                              21 DMI
   23.   ~(∃x)(Ax)                                          22 REP
```

3. 1. ~(∃x)(Mx · ~(x=j) · Cj)   Mjb?
   2. Ca · Mab · Sa
   3. (∀x)(Sx ⊃ Mx)
   4. Sa   2 Simp
   5. S(x) ⊃ M(x)   3 UI
   6. Sa ⊃ Ma   5 UN
   7. Ma   4,6 MP
   8. (∀x)~(Mx · ~(x=j) · Cx)   1 QE
   9. ~(M(x) · ~((x)=j) · C(x))   8 UI
   10. ~(Ma · ~(a=j) · Ca)   9 UN
   11. ~Ma v ~~(a=j) v ~Ca   10 DeM
   12. ~~(a=j) v ~ Ca   7,11 SC
   13. Ca   Simp
   14. ~~(a-j)   12,13 SC
   15. a=j   14 DN
   16. Mab   2 Simp
   17. Mjb   15,16 ID

5. 1. (∀x)((Kxa · ~(x=a)) ⊃ x=s)   (∃x)(~Px · ~Kxa)
   2. Ps · Pa · ~Pj
   3. (K(x)a · ~((x)=a)) ⊃ (x)=s   1 UI
   4. Ps   2 Simp
   5. ~Pj   2 Simp
   6. ~(s=j)   4,5 Neg ID
   7. ~(j=s)   6 Com Id
   8. (Kja · ~(j=a)) ⊃ j=s   3 UN
   9. ~(Kja · ~(j=a))   7,8 MT
   10. ~Kja v ~~(j=a)   9 DeM
   11. Pa   2 Simp
   12. ~(a=j)   5,11 Neg ID
   13. ~(j=a)   12 Com ID
   14. ~Kja   10,13 SC
   15. ~Pj · ~Kja   5,14 Conj
   16. ~P[x] · ~K[x]a   15 NP
   17. (∃x)(~Px · ~Kxa)   17 EG

7. 1. (∀x)(∀y)((Dx · Pyx) ⊃ y=a)
   2. (∀x)(∀y)((Dx · Eyx) ⊃ Pyx)
   3. (∀x)[Dx ⊃ (∃y)(∃z)(Eyx · Ezx · ~(z=a))]
   *4. (∃x)(Dx)   ACP
   *5. D[x]   4 EI
   *6. D(x) ⊃ (∃y)(∃z)(Ey(x) · Ez(x) · ~(y=z))   3 UI
   *7. D[x] ⊃ (∃y)(∃z)(Ey[x] · Ez[x] · ~(y=z))   6 UP
   *8. (∃y)(∃z)(Ey[x] · Ez[x] · ~(y=z))   5,7 MP
   *9. (∃z)(E[y][x] · E z [x] · ~([y]=z))]   8 EI
   *10. E[y][x] · E[z][x] · ~([y]=[z])   9 EI
   *11. (∀y)((D(x) · Ey(x)) ⊃ Py(x))   2 UI
   *12. (D(x) · E(y)(x)) ⊃ P(y)(x)   11 UI
   *13. (D[x] · E(y)[x]) ⊃ P(y)[x]   12 UP
   *15. (D[x] · E[y][x]) ⊃ P[y][x]   13 UP
   *16. E[y][x]   10 Simp
   *17. D[x] · E[y][x]   5,16 Conj
   *18. P[y][x]   15,17 MP
   *19. D[x] · P[y][x]   5,18 Conj
   *20. (∀y)((D(x) · Py(x)) ⊃ y=a)   1 UI
   *21. (D(x) · P(y)(x)) ⊃ (y)=a   20 UI
   *22. (D[x] · P(y)[x]) ⊃ (y)=a   21 UP
   *23. (D[x] · P[y][x]) ⊃ [y]=a   22 UP
   *24. [y]=a   19,23 MP
   *25. (D[x] · E[z][x]) ⊃ P[z][x]   13 UP
   *26. E[z][x]   10 Simp

101

*27.	D[x] · E[z][x]	5,26 Conj
*28.	P[z][x]	25,27 MP
*29.	D[x] · P[z][x]	5,28 Conj
*30.	(D[x] · P[z][x]) ⊃ [z]=a	22 UI
*31.	[z]=a	29,30 MP
*32.	a=[z]	31 Com Id
*33.	[y]=[z]	24,32 Trans Id
*34.	~([y]=[z])	10 Simp
*35.	[y]=[z] v ~(∃x)(Dx)	33 Add
*36.	~(∃x)(Dx)	34,35 SC
37.	(∃x)(Dx) ⊃ ~(∃x)(Dx)	4-36 RCP
38.	~(∃x)(Dx) v ~(∃x)(Dx)	37 DMI
39.	~(∃x)(Dx)	38 Rep